BLURRED AND KNOWN

BLURRED AND KNOWN

a journey through chaos

Ryan R. F. Wilkinson

iUniverse, Inc.
Bloomington

Blurred and Known
a journey through chaos

iUniverse books may be ordered through booksellers or by contacting:

iUniverse
1663 Liberty Drive
Bloomington, IN 47403
www.iuniverse.com
1-800-Authors (1-800-288-4677)

ISBN: 978-1-4759-3847-0 (sc)
ISBN: 978-1-4759-3848-7 (e)
ISBN: 978-1-4759-3849-4 (dj)

Library of Congress Control Number: 2012912873

Printed in the United States of America

iUniverse rev. date: 9/11/2012

I have found myself in a place of peace, and I have forever taken to the life before me. To all those who have been with me through challenges and success, thank you with all my heart.

Introduction

To anyone and everyone who decides to read this story, thank you. I will begin by saying that issues of family violence are very real. For millions of children and families around the world, family violence does exist. If you have the ability, the capacity and the compassion to find yourself in a helping situation, please take that step. Life should be about laughs, growth, relationships, celebrations of milestones, and the opportunity to reach potential through free will.

I am compelled to share this story to reach others who have lived this same life, to help, to inspire, and to link the idea of a better life. Hopefully, this book connects with those who have gone through, or who are going through similar events in their lives.

The story is told through a child's eyes as he grows into adulthood: his perspective, reflections, and thoughts on the events and the family turmoil he was a part of.

I hope that this book reaches those souls who search, endure, and trust that the other side is within reach. I offer my insight, with open arms to learn more.

Contents

How can you not hear the cries when they bury the laughter?
How can your words heal when time stands still hereafter?

How can you ignore the violence when it burns within our eyes?
Wrap your earth around me; I'm drowning in your lies

Clear skies in the distance, an arm's reach, a hand's resistance,
From the life that I once bled

Small hopes come and gone, overcast pushed and drawn
I will set the time to end this night

I will light the flame that burns this life
And above all,

I will cleanse this dish of bitter past
And find true passion that will last

1977

Birth

Are we given our smiles before we are born? Are they our shadows that follow, keeping our secrets? I have no place on earth like the one filled with peace in my own heart and mind. But I have to create this.

I don't remember being born. I remember nothing of it. As babies, we receive one thing constantly and immediately: love. As we get older, it gets complicated. Since I don't remember anything from infancy, I will fabricate it; I was happy, joyful, cranky, smelly, crying, hungry, ambitious, eager, curious, motivated, confident, loving, pure, safe, and full of life. My thoughts were new, and my thoughts were real. There were no tainted obstructions to adulterate my thoughts. For babies, nothing drives thoughts toward the sadness and pain that we all encounter later on in our lives.

My ears remained sharp to the sounds around me. My mouth exploded with sensation when I ate. My eyes took in the colours

1

and objects I was encapsulated by, and saliva dripped from my lips. My fingers tingled when they touched whatever it was I touched. My sleep was sound, deep, and invigorating. My worries were none, and I knew nothing of the world's horrible things. My world was simply my world. It was beautiful. But my vision of the future was somewhat blurred.

1982

Aware

I wondered. I continued to wonder and ponder. I felt pain, sadness, and loneliness early, wanting to understand the world with a profound appetite. I found peace in happy people. I gave everything I had into everything I did because I didn't think of consequence or failure. It was a constant awareness that helped me grow through the years. Antoine De Saint-Exupery said, "Grown-ups never understand anything for themselves, and it is tiresome for children to be always and forever explaining things to them." It took a particular wisdom stapled into the peripherals of my mind to understand that I was aware.

I reached out for a hug from my father. He hugged me back. I reached out for a hug from my grandmother. She hugged me back. *What a simple gesture*, I thought. It was effective and yet immensely rewarding on both ends.

I admired my older sister, and a few years later I would have a younger sister whom I also cherished. I started to take notice of other family members. Being five was interesting because I certainly found an awareness of life. It was a transition from being too young to comprehend, to a point when I was kicked in the face with the consciousness that life is happening around me. Things started to click. I began to wonder about the world. I asked my mother, "Does everyone have food?" She replied as if I had asked a silly question, "Yes, of course, Zechariah." I considered her answer but continued to wonder if it was really true. And of course, I would later realize that not everyone in the world eats every day. I formed my own opinions of my family, kids at school, and people in general. I took note of strangers. For adults, strangers go by so fast, but for children, strangers look at you with a smile. They pause, and take the time to wholeheartedly give energy and light. They smiled at me when I was young, but this seemed to fade as I got older, as if smiling could put you in prison. I have always felt warmth from people's friendliness, regardless if I knew them or not. When people were smiling around me, it put me in a different state of mind. It let me enjoy life without worry, angst, or fear. It helped open the door to letting me be me. Innocence emanates and surfaces when smiles are offered. What would life be like if we always smiled?

For some reason, we moved a lot, always settling in and then picking up over and over again. It felt like we were running all the time. Of course, at that age, I just followed along and didn't really have a choice in what happened. I remember lots of boxes packed high to the ceiling every time we moved.

My parents had divorced when I was two and remarried other partners when I was six. The way I was raised was not guided or instructed, but rather loose. This means that there was no strict structure in place helping to form who I should have become. Nor should there really be, but guidance would have been welcomed. "Mom, can I go down to the store to get some sports cards?" "Sure, don't be long," she said, even though the store was two blocks away and I was only six. It's amazing how times have changed over the years. I was given no instruction on how to be or on what to do with my life. Is there ever really instruction, for anyone? I had only the reality around me as I watched and soaked it all in. I learned by observation, and I failed through application most times. I eventually thought, of course, that I knew everything, but this would be curbed later in life by humiliation and reality. I learned from my parents, and they learned from their parents, and so on. At that age, we can't choose our surroundings; we only see and hear what is presented in front of us. That's where I eventually found a bit of madness. The madness was learned. I knew something was going on outside of my immediate world, and I knew that I was interested, curious, and in need of something more. I knew what I saw at times was not right.

With awareness, I've always agreed it's good to admit mistakes, and at times it's alright to hide the truth to protect your children. What isn't alright is to take away an environment that's conducive to a child reaching his potential. Sometimes I would notice people with a mentality built from walls. They would be closed off to the outside world and what was really going on around them. To have that mindset is to be behind a road block. Children, as we know, have an uncanny ability to develop and grow their minds at a fast rate. Imagine what we can learn from a child. We can learn as much from them as they can learn from others, if not more. Regardless of the age gap, imagine what we can take away from them every day if we open our minds. Imagine the exchange that could take place. Children look at the world through the eyes of original innocence. I was wise to it. Sometimes we don't see ourselves as individuals in tune with awareness, but as individuals in line with society, obsolete of original thought. But children are aware. Children are deep thinkers, who constantly grow through soaking in the elements around them. I was aware.

It was 9:09 on a Tuesday morning. My mother quietly walked over and sat down beside me on the couch. I was lying across two cushions and she sat at the end, lifted my feet, and put them back on top of her legs. I was not talking but staring at the television that was making noise with daytime game shows. "Zechariah, you need to eat breakfast; how about some eggs?" my mother whispered. I shook my head and started drifting to sleep. I was sick with the flu. It was day five. As my fever regressed, I had asked for some toast on day four, but that was all. It was a hard flu. I had watched enough television to sustain me for months. I looked up at my mother and asked, "Why are all these people pretending?" My mother looked at the television, then back at me, and told me it was all just for laughs anyway. I agreed that since they were all in a small box, they may have gone crazy. I chuckled at my thoughts and was aware of how silly and sick I was at the same time.

As much as I could recollect as a child, when I became an adult, memories of childhood surroundings became insurmountable, like short films constantly flashing before me. When they were bad short films, as time went on, I felt they should become photos stored in unopened photo albums. What if the movies kept playing over and over again in my mind? What if the movies were horror movies? What if I couldn't put them away forever?

My life bulb was shining bright early in my life. My eyes were opened as I saw dark places that had the possibility of being filled with fear. My awareness allowed me to understand my surroundings. I realized I could bring this awareness into everything I did and adapt to new surroundings. It eventually let me understand who I was, who I could become, and what I could do for others. When I was one with my surroundings and myself, I was aware.

1983

Ethics

I always wondered why my life unfolded the way it did. I thought about the people and events which had the most impact in my life. Was it really so hard to find someone who could show me the way, show me how I was supposed to act, feel, grow, and be? Struggle came when I had no one to guide me, no one to look at, and no one to help make me feel that everything would unfold as it should. I had no one to tell me that I would ultimately be safe. The struggle of finding the right path, of creating my own self, came at a price. Even more so, it took great effort to find my morals and ethics along the way. I can't help but think we are all connected, with our souls passing through each other and our minds locked in an unconscious state. Face it: we are all alike in some way. We are all one, though at times we are lost in a world of no one, wearing masks. Ethics were important to sustain my growth and form me into someone who was not alone.

It was another Tuesday morning around 8:09. My stepdad decided to take the training wheels off my bike. "Ready,

Zechariah?" I nodded hard with a big smile on my face. He ran beside me as I pedaled and then he let go. My hands gripped the handle bars, my teeth clenched, and my little legs moved as fast as they could. The bike wobbled and I took a nasty spill. The training wheels went back on.

When I was six, my mother, sister, and I lived with my grandparents. The house was very warm and inviting. My grandparents were rich in their traditions. My grandfather was a well known painter. His art held such originality. With each passing year, his paintings resembled the growing maturation of his soul, and his journey poured out on the canvas. The colours gave glimpses into his love for life. His timeless art took me from as early as the forties to modern day. He also carved wood, although rarely. Through the years I tried my best to emulate his work, using vibrant colours, heart, history, and most of all, passion. For so many, art is a demonstration of love and life experience, and I was attempting to understand that. Above all my grandfather was one of the most inspirational men in my life. He knew what life was about, he laughed and smiled, worked hard, and provided for a family the way a man should. He was a man because he believed in himself. He had integrity as a father, a grandfather, a husband, and a friend. He was always smiling, no matter the situation.

My grandfather never got angry with me, except once. I was at their cottage pushing my little sister in a stroller very quickly along a gravel driveway. I flipped over her and landed on the back of the stroller, smashing her face into the gravel and knocking out a tooth. My grandfather ran over, helped us up, and was quick to ask, "What are you thinking? Why are you doing that with your sister?" This was the only time he ever raised his voice at me. I understood his point very clearly, and began to apply more logic to what I did.

My grandmother was always so caring and loving. She admired my grandfather, supported him in his life's passions, and they complimented each other perfectly. There was always adoration and admiration for each other sparkling in their eyes. I thought what they had was rare, and it turned out to be true.

I was fortunate to have two sets of grandparents whose lives reflected bravery, honour, and ethics. They were unique, caring, interested, warm, and always full of love. I formed a particular closeness to my grandfather on my mother's side, probably because I lived around them the most. He taught me the importance of ethics and how to use discipline to structure the way I lived. I paid close attention to my grandparents; they instilled my values.

My father's parents were similar to my mother's parents. As role models, they set examples that I could emulate, which were important in defining who I became. For my grandfather on my father's side, what stands out for me was his ability to learn and adapt. He was honest and dedicated to his family. He always knew how important ethics and morals were to a good life. I needed them to complete the structure that was vital to my existence. If I was to be happy, I needed a foundation to take me there. My father's mother was pure and kind, and I do not recall a time when she wasn't putting others first. Her spirit has always soared through me and her smile remains in my thoughts. In fact, both my grandmothers were remarkable women who stood beside their families and were honest, caring, and loyal to the ones they loved. I always felt I needed more people like them in my life.

One late night at my grandparents' house, my cousin and I were searching through the mountain of toys on my bedroom floor when she looked at me blankly. "Who is that?" she whispered. "Who is who?" I whispered back. She pointed at the window and I turned to look. In the window was a man's face. It was wrinkled and dark. The face looked like it had been carved from wood, old and aged, reminding me of an old soul holding on to what little life was left. The face had no emotion, nor did it move in any way. The face continued to look at us and we continued to look at it. It reminded me of an old Native Indian, lost in his journey, lost in the new era and struggling to find his way. I felt slightly scared, sad, and somewhat excited that this was happening. I was too young to really understand the 'spirituality' of the event. We didn't rush, but slowly went to find our grandparents. "There was a face in the window, a face in the window!" I said jumping up and down. My cousin piped in, "There was a man's face in the window!" while pointing to my room. They didn't seem impressed and just looked at us with puzzled expressions. My grandfather went to my room, took a quick peek and said, "See, no one is here but you two." Were we seeing things? Did the face in the window have meaning? Why did we both see it? It was years later that my cousin and I talked again about the face to get confirmation. We still wondered why it had been there, who he was, and what journey was unfolding for him. From a young age, my cousin was always a fun happy girl, full of laughter and inspiration. She was one of the most honest and pure hearted people I knew. It would have made no sense for her to be a story teller. We were still so young and pure when we saw the face; however, maybe our story was a bit much for our grandparents, and if it was too much for them, why would we tell anyone else?

One Sunday morning as I was riding my bike, the neighbours told me that my training wheels weren't even touching the road. So they convinced me to take them off. Actually, they took them off. Sure enough, when I got back on my bike, I rode without training wheels. I didn't need any assistance in helping me rush through the air and pedal freely on the road. I remember smiling from ear to ear until my mother came out and was upset at the neighbour kids. "Zechariah, what are you doing? Why did you take the wheels off? You could get hurt!" she yelled. Was she mad because she hadn't helped me, and had missed the moment? I looked at her and happily said, "But, Mom, I wanted to show you I could do it on my own." A slow mirroring smile began to stretch across her face. "I knew you could do it on your own, Zechariah!" she replied.

I knew I was beginning to ride life on my own. The ethics and values I had been forming were starting to roll. I looked down at my bike, proud and knowingly absent of training wheels, and then I looked over at the front window to see my grandmother smiling and waving. She was proud of me, and I was happy to see her face in the window.

1984

Reality

Thinking deeply can really spin our minds. Our thoughts can lead us in multiple directions. Our thoughts can distort and blur reality. Our thoughts can bring demons if we let them. It's only when we have control over our thoughts that we can nurture them toward good or bad. It's really our own choosing. Otherwise there are other forces at work, coercing us in uncertain directions. Our past can become elastic, and distort and blur our reality. At times it can hold us back, cause tension, and add weight. It can paralyze us. We have the ability to bring foresight into our lives if we take the time to reflect on our past and propel clarity to our future. We have the ability to envision something real and we can achieve deep thoughts that slowly become our reality. Or, our minds can gradually become our prison.

I was walking down the street; it was dark, with the glaring wetness of newly dropped rain. As I turned the corner, I could see the department store, and people running. Screams filled the streets as I walked closer with a rising interest. I froze suddenly and just watched. I heard two gun shots, close. *I have got to move*, I thought to myself. *"Zechariah, move!"* For some reason, I ran toward the store, against the people running in the opposite direction. Then I saw him, the gunman, standing tall in the darkness. I could see the streetlight reflecting off his gun. I ran straight into the store, pretty sure the gunman saw me. Although he walked, and I ran, his walking speed was just as fast as my running speed. *"Where to go? Where to go?"* I repeatedly asked myself. I saw a circular rack of clothing out on the open floor. I jumped into the middle of it, and waited. The screams had diminished and I couldn't hear much of anything. There was so much silence after so much noise. *Do I peek out? Do I get up?* Then I felt something cold and metallic pressing against my head… click. At 1:09 in the morning, I awoke. It wasn't real, but I would have this dream a number of times.

A few nights later at 12:09 in the morning, I was watching a favourite movie. I had asked my mother if I could stay up and watch, and to my surprise she said yes. I watched into the early hours of the morning, my pillow against the leg of the coffee table, and my body sprawled out in front of the television. As I lay engulfed in the movie, every so often I became preoccupied by my surroundings. At times it got cold. At times it got colder. I began to look around the living room, over to the stairs and through the hallway at nothing. My peripheral vision caught glimpses of shadows and my heart started to pound. I wasn't tired and I wasn't too interested in the movie anymore at this point. I moved my pillow to the couch and backed my body into the corner cushion in full sight of the room. The sound of the movie began to dissipate as the sound of footsteps got louder. I lay frozen on the couch in a stare of complete numbness. As the noise grew closer and closer I managed to move. My right foot planted on the ground and my fists clenched. *"Go!"* I screamed in my mind, then bang! I was off running. As I approached my room, I had to first go past the stairs that led to the basement. I recall a darker shadow, tall, still, and angry, looking up at me with no face. I ran up the stairs and into my bedroom. I was under the covers, head peeking out, eyes wide open, and my ears paying full attention to the sound of the footsteps coming up the stairs. My bed was beside the door so my head was in immediate reach of anything that was to come in. I screamed. My mother screamed, "Zechariah! What's going on?" as she ran in to the bedroom. I looked at her and immediately unleashed tears down my face.

I used to watch cartoons in the basement of that same house. The basement was dark, and at least in my youthful mind, evil. It was far from reality. The basement was partially a crawl space filled with boxes of old toys. It had pull chain lights, nooks, and crannies that created a dark maze. Anytime I went down there to watch television, I ran to the couch and ran back upstairs only to feel the grasps of hands at my back and the breath of whatever it was behind me. More of my imagination got the best of me and I began to show signs of fear and fright through my attitude. Hallowe'en was soon approaching and I was going to be a gorilla. My older sister didn't know about my costume, so I decided to play a prank on her. The gorilla mask was very lifelike with coarse hair sweeping around the head of the mask. One early morning I snuck into my sister's room, my head peeking over the bed at the side. I put the mask on, poked her side, and she rolled over with her eyes still closed. I tapped her shoulder and called her name quietly. Her eyes opened slowly and I just sat there, saying nothing until I let out a big growl! She screamed, stood up on the bed, and screamed again. My mother ran in to see what was going on, and I removed the mask. Tears first appeared in my sister's eyes, but they quickly changed to laughter and then she threw a big punch to my arm.

By April my mother had grown more concerned over my poor behaviour, dreams, fear, and paranoia and decided that a child therapist would be a solution. We arrived at the building and walked in and up a long staircase. "Zechariah, wait here while I talk with the doctor," my mother said. I nodded. Even in the waiting room, sitting alone, I managed to hear footsteps slowly climbing up the stairs. I panicked and crazily knocked on the office door. I don't remember the conversations with the therapist; however, I do remember the visions along the way and the recurring nightmares that ensued. My visions would depict skeletons standing around my bed, leaning over me, watching and twisting their heads. Footsteps of more skeletons would come up the stairs until they joined the others in my room. Their faces were dark, void of light yet alive. My spirit was turning and the days grew darker. I even threatened suicide after I spilled juice on the floor. "I am going to kill myself!" My mother paused, and then asked, "How are you going to do that?" I scrunched my face up and yelled back, "I am going to take a knife and stab myself in the stomach!"

The demons turned to rage for me. I began to project my fear outward, toward others. I did things I wouldn't normally do and my behaviour was constantly poor. I would hold onto this for quite some time because they were the demons I had chosen. They were the demons I accepted. Two years of fear passed through me in this house. Two years of creating demons, and learning that the world was not as nice as it first appeared to be. I turned into an angry child. I hit other kids, trapped them behind doors, and used profanity when I talked. My mindset was to always trick, twist, and contort others around me into doing what I wanted. I spoke out in class at school and I stole from family. I think at that point in my life I was starting to become aware of what was defining me.

Where would I turn? Which direction would I take? What was real and what wasn't? I was lost in the middle. I was searching for the reality that I wanted. What reality did I want? How could I know at such a young age? "Zechariah?" my mother asked. "Yah," I responded. "Let's talk for a bit about what is happening with you," she said, concerned. I looked up at her, put my toy down, and said, "I'm angry Mom." "I know you are and I want to tell you that it's okay. And I want you to imagine one of your superheroes punching those skeletons the next time they come see you," she said. I looked at the floor, then back up to her, and smiled. "I will."

At 5:09 that evening the sun was disappearing around the earth. Music played in the background from another room while my mother muddled around. I was in the living room on the floor near the window, staring out at the sun. My mother walked over to me and quietly asked, "Zechariah, are you hungry?" I shook my head and continued to look at the setting sun. There was warmth that night, from the sun, from my mother, and from the peace that was for the moment, in me. I focused on it. I learned from it. It was the calm before the storm that would soon approach me, a moment in time when I realized that what was happening around me was real. I eventually escaped some of my own demons, yet what awaited me were the demons of others.

I began to see that the world is very different, and can turn very ugly when hate leads thought. I never completely gave into hate. However, to find reality, sometimes I needed to hang with the demons before I could fly with the angels.

1985

Attitude

I stood in a field outside the school and stared into the distance. The wind blew around me, sweeping past my feet and through my hair. My eyes were half closed from the sun hitting my face. I knew I could do it. I believed in myself. I drew in a deep breath, and started running. My legs contracted and my arms moved back and forth along the way. I ran. I ran fast and then I jumped. At first, my arms swung out in front of me, and then my feet soon lifted off the ground. It was difficult to push hard enough to really take off. But there I was, flying. And then I awoke. My life's dream as a child was to fly. I wanted to fly through the air and thought that if I could fly I would be free. I knew I could lift off and fly toward a great life. My life was always like a giant waiting room. I sat in it, waiting for something to happen. Sometimes I would make something happen, and the rest of the time I would sit in a paralyzed state of mind, waiting. But when I took off, I knew I could fly. What was I waiting for? I was waiting for my attitude to change.

Dreams are to life like air is to lungs. Sure, that's a bold statement. If we don't dream, we don't aspire. We don't hope. Dreams can help define our attitude. They keep us unique and original. Everyone wants to be different in this world. Everyone wants to be original and authentic. And when I say dream, I mean our waking dreams, not the ones we have when we sleep.

I sat on a bench in a park two blocks from my home. It was 2:09 in the afternoon. A young couple sat on the other side. My mother looked down at me and said, "Zechariah, wipe your face." I was eating a chocolate ice cream cone. I looked back at her and said, "But I will just make another mess." My mother clamoured and said, "Better to clean a small mess than a big one." *How true,* I thought. But really, it seemed to me that she was embarrassed of me having chocolate ice cream all over my face in front of strangers. I was a child, so in my opinion a messy face was fine. We set out toward home and continued walking, eating our ice cream. My mother was quiet on this day but warm with love. On our way home I heard my mother finally mumble a few words, "Hope he isn't home when we get there." I looked up at her, confused, and she put her hand on my head. When we got home my stepfather was sitting watching television. My mother spoke loudly, "I can smell it on your breath, you know," as she stared at him. He glanced over at her and said nothing. I stood, confused and interested at the same time. His attitude toward my mother was changing. He was significantly abrupt, confrontational, and removed from our family as time pushed on. I was often confused about what kind of relationship they had. I often wondered why they were together and I often wondered what love was shared between them. The feeling I sensed was toxic. But what did I know at my age about relationships?

1985 delivered my younger sister into the world, and this was something that brought me great joy and happiness. Her birth changed my outlook and my attitude. I started looking more closely at how I could respond to things in my life. Sometimes I would respond poorly, and sometimes I would respond with deep thought and careful approach. When she was born, it opened up my eyes into how special a baby can be: inviting, full of life, and so close to a pure soul. My attitude changed for the better because of her birth. I started to smile more. I started to understand more closely that my attitude could help me have a better life. I began to understand that my attitude was a choice, which would ultimately define who I was going to be.

Viktor E. Frankl describes his life in hellish surroundings, and his decision to emerge by using his mind, choices, and attitude. Frankl talks about the ability to choose one's attitude in any given set of circumstances, and how it is one of our last human freedoms. Frankl chronicles his experience as a concentration camp inmate in his book *Man's Search for Meaning*, and describes his method of finding a reason to live within his attitude. He thought his way through the worst of times that anyone could ever imagine, smiling until the end. I thought of this story as unbelievable, remarkable, and inspiring. I knew that people had experienced worse than what I was used to, and acceptance of these other stories was part of my reasoning to pursue happiness. Although, when exactly I would find that happiness was certainly a mystery to me. However, my attitude would define how positive I would be in any given situation, no matter what life had for me. I wanted to challenge the meaning of life, like Frankl did. I wanted to always wonder and pursue until I had answers and internal contentment. My attitude would help me if I remained positive, pure to my values, and solid in thought. Frankl chose to turn tragedy into a positive, because he had internal hope and purpose in his life regardless of where he was or what he was doing. Imagine, the ability to define attitude and to have it carry you through the most traumatic period in life. Nothing supersedes that and nothing ever would, in my mind. What Frankl went through and what he overcame was sensational. His true human spirit was based solely on a chosen attitude.

I knew I was in a position to choose my own attitude. I never wanted anyone else to define it for me. The more years that passed, the more I realized how attitude impacted my life. Attitude seemed to define the amount of energy I had. My attitude was more important than what other people thought or did, it was more important than appearance, and it was certainly more important than popularity. It was more important than money, possessions, and other superficial things that controlled my life at certain times. Remarkably, we have a choice every day regarding the attitude we will embrace. My attitude defined me mentally or broke me down if I let it. We are each in control of our attitudes above anything else, and we have the power to distinguish how we react to anything that comes our way in this world. It took me a while to digest the thought of attitude and really break it down into an understandable concept. I found that words such as 'attitude' which carried such power can simply be words, or we can choose to have those words carry out meaning and action. The meaning can resonate through us, driving us to take action, but only if we really connect to it. We can become those words through our minds. We can become those words through our spirit.

"You sit there and don't move until you want to say sorry to your sister," my mother said. "I don't want to say sorry. She hit me first!" I yelled back. My mother stared and then sat down. She put her arm around me and said, "Zechariah, sometimes it doesn't matter who did what. Sometimes it's about doing the right thing. When we do the right thing it can change our attitude." I sat there quietly. I continued to look at the carpet and digest what my mother had said. Though I didn't quite understand it at the time, it sure hit me hard later in life. Her words helped me see beyond the current moment.

I soon realized there were a number of people in this world who had particularly horrible attitudes. The negativity and self consumption of people, I realized, can drain us. It can take us away from everything else in our life. We are constantly giving those people energy that could be put elsewhere. We can decide who we want to give that energy to. We can give it to people that deserve it. We can give it to ourselves. Put the energy into something good. Put it into something rewarding and energizing. When we choose where it goes, we can choose to place our energy into an attitude that will ultimately define our lives or even our legacy.

Attitude was and still remains vital in my life. It guides me and helps me see the right direction. Choosing my attitude was a fundamental part of my existence, my thoughts, and my soul. When I chose my attitude, I soon realized I was choosing who I was going to be.

1986

Failure

It is with great failure that we reach great understanding. Failure to me was an attempt made, a lesson learned, and wisdom gained. Failure was essential to success. The programming of the human mind begins at birth from our surroundings and is cultivated through failure. It's interesting how our lives get laid out before us like an outfit. For some, the impact of irrelevant failure will forever change their direction. Hopefully, we can weed out those irrelevancies and find the important pieces. People, society, school, and television can all program us to think ill of failure if we allow them to. The idea that we cannot fail in life is ridiculous and fictional. It is through failure that we learn, we grow, and we become amiable in our approach to life. We have to. We have to adapt to failure. We need to embrace failure.

My father continued to encourage me as I splashed into and out of the water. It was 1:09 in the afternoon and we were out on the lake. The wind was strong that day and we were both wearing life jackets for our safety. I was thankful for mine because I had already spent an hour in the water and was growing tired and weak. My father was teaching me to windsurf. I was trying to pull the sail out of the water while attempting to balance on the board. I would get it halfway, sometimes almost up, and then I would let go. I only wanted to succeed for my father that day, no one else. As he demonstrated how to do it, I watched with intensity and perseverance. As I made what seemed to be the ninetieth attempt, I fell back into the water, releasing the sail. The water covered my tears and my father didn't notice. He asked me once again to try, but by that time my arms were too weak. I asked him if we could go back to the cottage. "Of course, Zechariah," he said with a smile. He made sure I was sitting securely on the back of the board as he lifted the sail. He looked back at me, smiled again, and asked if I was ready. I gave a nod and off we went. When we got back to the cottage everyone asked how I did. Before I said a word my father jumped in: "He did very well and he almost pulled the sail right up out of the water. Considering it's a large size sail that most adults couldn't pull up, I'm quite impressed." The smile stretched across my face and I found an excitement within. He never got mad, never spoke an ill word, and never gave up on me. To him, I didn't fail, but only succeeded, and he made sure I knew.

Many people say that change can be a good thing. I believe change brings new beginnings, but also failure. The past will always leave footprints, and always be a part of us, and that includes failure. We seem to remember our failures more than our successes. All of us have a past that sometimes whispers in our ears. Some people's pasts whisper more often than others. Some of our pasts scream at us, while other pasts smile back. And again, there is always worse out there. When we understand this, we accept responsibility in our lives. We accept responsibility for who we are and what we do. To really accept life for the time it occurs, we must find common ground with others. We want acceptance, and we want peace of mind that we will be cared about. We must accept death, love, hate, sadness, and happiness in order to find our true meaning, through the reality of failure. That meaning is whatever we want to create. We should all have our own creations of meaning. We have the freedom to do so. I didn't find my meaning early. I never believed that there was a specific time for this. Most times we are too caught up in finding meaning when we should just focus on our lives as they are. I read once that life has a destiny for each of us, but a tension of opposites is created because we want to do something else. I had many moments in my life where I stood still, wondering what was next: darkness or light. There were many of those moments and the darkness never stopped pushing and pulling.

Along the way of discovering failure, I wanted to continue finding meaning. Meaning is something that gradually comes together like a jigsaw puzzle. When we try and stamp a piece into the wrong place, we learn from that mistake, learning not to force life, but let it unfold naturally. From this experience, we have built part of our meaning. Meaning is really our own definition, so I knew I could not let someone else define my meaning for me. I needed to define it. I needed to live it on my own terms and be proud of it. I needed to be me even if I thought the meaning of life was to fail and learn over and over again. I always felt I needed to suffer and fail in order to achieve peace and contentment. I needed to suffer in order to appreciate. When I failed, there was a pain that came with it. When I understood the failure, the pain was released. I was wrong many times over. And I will always be wrong in many circumstances. However, being wrong sometimes also meant please show me the way, and I will do my best to do the right thing next time. If I wasn't shown, then I would learn through more failure.

Midway through the 1986 school year, report cards came out. My teacher handed mine to me and I quickly gazed over the grades and felt my stomach sink. The two-block walk home was a long one. I focused on the ground and watched each foot plant in front of the other. The ground was dirty and the air was warm. The sounds around me vanished and all I heard was each of my pant legs scuffing together. My thoughts were scrambled. I eventually arrived home, report card in hand. I walked in the basement door, quietly made my way past my mother's room, and went upstairs to my own room. I sat on the bed and looked at the report card again. My eyes couldn't change the fact of what I saw on that paper. Not doing anything about it wouldn't prevent it from being there. My mother entered the room and I immediately started to cry. She sat on the bed, placed her arm around me, and asked what was going on. I felt embarrassed, ashamed, and at the time, like my world had ended. "Zechariah, what happened?" "I got an F in math, Mom. I'm sorry." My mother looked at me; her eyes filled with compassion, and provided words that eventually put a smile on my face. "Zechariah, your life will be filled with failure, and that's okay. It's really how you accept failure and what you do about it that will help you learn to be a better you," she softly said. While I was someone who never wanted to fail and be the best, there was inevitably going to be a time when I did fail. I knew I had failed in math, but at the same time it was clear that I had gained so much more.

I would grow to understand that without failure, you didn't succeed. Michael Jordan talked about how many shots he missed in his basketball career, and how many shots he missed in a game. Although he was entrusted to take game winning shots, he missed many. Jordan talked about how many times he failed, over and over again in his life, and said that was ultimately how he was able to succeed. This is a wise point, and it resonated through to my understanding that if we don't make the attempt, success would possibly never come. I realized that in life I needed to at least make an attempt, an attempt to succeed or even an attempt to fail. If I failed, then I was actually learning and growing. How could I not want to fail? If I fail, then I am that much closer to having success. I needed to invest in my failure. Failure was something I would embrace.

1987

Peace

Connect the dots. We draw a line from each event in our lives and connect the dots. The picture we are left with is up to us. Is it a picture of our selves? Is it a picture of our family? Is the picture a beach with the ocean transparent in the sun? Maybe the picture is a giant mess. Maybe the picture is an abstract of life events. Perhaps the picture is an abstract of our mind, chaotic and uncontrolled. Or maybe it's a picture of fear, with hope in the distance. Hopefully at the end it's a picture of peace.

Part of my world was being a kid; the other part was being an adult. We moved to a new house and another new beginning. I tried not to complicate things but that was my nature. My madness dictated my thoughts. Some days these complications would cease, and then peace would peek at me, become stronger, not hiding away in the distance.

It was 10:09 in the morning in the month of September and I was in grade five at a new school. The curriculum in my previous school was actually advanced, so I felt I was ahead. I sat in my desk while the teacher asked questions, and I looked around waiting to see if anyone other than me had the answer. I put my hand up. "Zechariah?" my teacher asked. I answered question after question until it happened. "Zechariah?" my teacher asked again. I answered the question with what I thought was the answer. It was wrong. I argued it, over and over again. As the argument took place I could feel my mouth becoming dry, my hands tightening their grip around the edges of the desk, and my eyes fixating on my teacher. "You think you know everything but you don't!" my teacher yelled. The classroom stood still. I shifted my eyes to the chalkboard and shut my mouth. Those words echoed through my head for days and I kept quiet for years.

Peace was faltering as I got older. The house I lived in became more absent of peace as the days and years went by. On a cold morning I awoke to a thunderous yell. It startled me and I forgot where I was. This seemed to be going on a lot lately and I was confused why it was happening. I had heard them yelling before and thought nothing of it, but now I could hear the defining words that tipped the building blocks of chaos. Usually the argument was about alcohol or money. But this time it was about how selfish my stepfather was being. We had moved many times by now and my mother was growing tired of it. I lay in bed, confused but angry, and I had enough. I walked out of my room toward the kitchen. There he was, sitting at the table, my mother nowhere to be found. I grabbed an empty beer bottle and lifted it near his head. "This is the reason this happens," I spurted intensely. His red eyes peered at me and his unpredictable essence reeked off him with the booze. "It's your mother who does this," he explained with a quiet mumble. I put the bottle down, shook my head, walked back to my room and locked the door, wondering if he would break through and come at me.

Early the next morning I walked into my mother's room to see her frantically packing bags. I asked, "Mom, what are you doing?" She stopped, sat on the bed, and looked me in the eyes. "Go grab some clothes Zechariah, and tell your sister to do the same." Ten minutes later she had my little sister in her arms and asked if we were ready. We all got in the car and sped off. We drove for a while, not sure where we'd end up, but we drove until my mother broke down and stopped the car on the side of the road. "Where are we going, Mom?" I asked. My mother looked at me, and then looked at my older sister, but with empty eyes. She paused for a moment and then started the car. It was like we weren't even in the car with her. I watched as her mind scattered around aimlessly, dormant and then vibrating again. I could see her struggling to make the decision, trying to find her soul and listen to what it was telling her. Her soul was struggling to rationalize through emotional conflict and logical vacancy. And then we went back to the same place we had left.

I stood in the hallway on the large navy ship. It was dark, and damp. I was walking toward the deck when the alarm sounded. It was loud, repetitive, and very irritating. "We are at war!" yelled another soldier. The hallways were darker than normal, with red lights flashing everywhere. The intercom speaker squealed, and then a voice was heard on the microphone, "Please get ready for all firearms unload." I back pedaled to the wall, staring at the red lights flashing, bracing myself. I looked to the end of the hallway where there was a payphone. I made my way over to it and called my wife, "Hey, it's Zechariah, we are at war, but I'll be alright. I love you so much." I could feel the ship starting to engage in fire, and spin. It started slowly, so I had time to brace myself with the palms of my hands flat against the wall. The weight increased as the ship spun faster and faster and I could feel the pressure against my body. The ship was shooting at all the surrounding enemies. The velocity became too much to bear, and I sacrificed myself to the pull of gravity. I tried to reach out in front of me but I couldn't, and I felt my body pressing against the wall to almost an unbearable pressure. The red lights flashing at a constant were the only things keeping me conscious. Then the red lights went out. And the ship slowed. As it came to a stop, there was silence. I made it out onto the deck to see destruction everywhere. Smoke, haze, an orange sky, and murky water had wrapped around me. Every breath filled my lungs with smoke from the guns. My eyes half closed with a sharp sting. But I was safe. I also had this dream a number of times. *So strange*, I thought. What did this dream mean? Life throws so much resistance at us. Sometimes it felt as though I would never be at peace, but I would later realize that peace comes from within. It was to come from a deep place in my gut, heart, and in my thoughts. It was something I had to build from scratch, regardless of the resistance in front of me. Resistance will never stop. But to find peace along the way makes it that much easier.

I was growing afraid of my parents. I felt broken and depleted. Every night the noise got louder, the fights grew stronger, and my fear prevailed. It was very awkward when my parents drank and argued, as if they were strangers and I had to adjust on the fly. I had to tiptoe around them, please them, cater to them and respond carefully; otherwise I knew what was coming. At ten years of age, I couldn't be myself around my parents. They suppressed my true personality because I felt I had to be someone different around them every time they were drinking, or else the chaos ensued. These situations invoked constant fear of the unknown. In our youth, we continue to develop who we are through our parents.

Meeting with chaos instead of peace deflects who we were truly meant to be. It altered me for life.

The next night I ran to the neighbours. I ran across the backyard as the dark dewy grass blurred past me. I ran so fast that I didn't take one breath until I reached my destination. I knocked on the door viciously until they answered. "Please, my mother is getting hurt, he won't stop, please, I need to call the cops," I said, while trying to catch my breath. The neighbours took me in, and I called the police. When these events happened, sometimes the neighbours would come over to our house, and sometimes I would run over to theirs.

For a few early years in the summers of my life we rented a cabin at a resort on the lake several hours from where we lived. At this resort they had an entertainment cabin for the kids to hang out, with video games and pool tables. At night we could make a campfire along the beach and during the day we could play basketball, badminton, or just hang out in the water. Our neighbours, the ones I ran to at night when horror would strike, rented a cabin nearby around the same time. I always wondered what they thought of us, because at one instance it would be chaos, but then we'd all get up the next day and be 'normal.' My neighbours had a son who was a year older than I was, and we hung out from time to time.

One summer he stayed with us in our cabin and slept in my room. My heart raced most of the night. My anxiety increased. It was a different atmosphere and different environment, so I wondered if the chaos would continue, and I wondered if it would continue in front of my friend. Could it happen? We fell asleep just before midnight and I awoke to some light talking out in the kitchen. I lay on my back, staring at the wall, my heart starting to beat faster and hoping that was all it was. The voices got louder and I became more nervous. I was hoping my friend would stay sleeping, but he woke up. I didn't know what to say except, "I think they are just joking." That wasn't the case at all. I could hear the table slide across the floor and then the screams. My friend sat up in his bed, wide eyed and scared, and I told him it was alright, nothing was going to happen to him. But I didn't completely believe my own words. I started to panic. I walked out to the kitchen and my nerves shot through my body like pure adrenaline. I looked at the table against the wall and then moved my eyes to him holding my mother by her neck. My thoughts raced because I didn't want my friend to come see what was going on. I wouldn't know how to respond to his questions. I asked my stepfather to please let her go. And that's when there was a knock on the door and they walked in. It was our neighbours, confused and horrified by what they were seeing. My friend's father grabbed my stepfather and pushed him back against the wall, and my friend's mother asked, "Where is my son?" I pointed to the room. She walked out of the cabin with him in her arms and left immediately. I don't recall what happened after that but I do recall how I felt the next day: embarrassed, confused, and sad. My friend was being taken from me. The truth of the matter was that I was prepared to lose friends before I gained them.

About a year later, it all came to an end one night when the neighbours' door was shut in my face. Our neighbours had finally had enough, and didn't want to be involved anymore. I could see them struggling to help every time, and the pain they felt while involved. I couldn't blame them for stopping. As the door shut behind me, I sat on their front steps, holding my face, tears leaking through the cracks of my fingers. There was nowhere to run, nowhere to hide, no one to help. I walked back to our house, slowly, in a daze, and reentered the madness.

Through these events I realized that peace was amiss. Peace was something I knew was achievable. I knew I wanted peace in my life, but I didn't want to spend my life searching for peace; I wanted to live in peace. I had to garner it on my own and cultivate it. I was never exposed to peace as much as I should have been. I knew peace could be bound to me by the foundation of good people; it could be grown in my soul and pursued until the remaining parts of my life created it. Peace was attainable if I really wanted it.

The drive took me onto a narrow dirt road full of sharp bends. If there was another car we'd pull over half into the ditch and shrubs to let it pass. In the fall the leaves of red, orange, yellow, and brown would wrap around us, encasing us in a tunnel of glowing colour. As we pulled up closer, I saw a small bungalow home, brown, with stone on the end wall and siding on the rest. When I say home, I mean home as in a place a family could be at peace. This particular home was full of history. It was a cottage at first, and eventually became my grandparents' retirement home. It became a shrine of my grandfather's art. The boathouse became his studio. When we pulled up, this home sparked an instant smile. When I got out of the car, I would take a deep breath. The air was crisp and clean, and a cool breeze collected around me. As I looked toward the home, I could see it was surrounded by water. On the property there were trees and flowers everywhere. On the corner to the right, there grew a large willow tree about fifteen feet from the house. There were two docks on each side, and a view of water and trees at the shore. It was beautiful. The sounds were that of the wind, water, and various birds who sang when the weather was good. As I came to the door, the sweetest grandparents would greet me. As I stepped into the home I would notice the smell of delicious roast beef and apple crisp cooking for dinner. Classical music played in the background and my grandfather's paintings hung on every wall. My ritual was to always walk around and look at the paintings with each visit. Then I would sit and take in the sounds and watch my family. Eventually I would wander outside again, absorbing more of the surroundings. When I was there, I could always see a bit more clearly. This was my peace.

1988

Amiable

The difference in my life at this point was that I knew change was constant. In order to accept change I knew I needed to install a missing component. I needed to be amiable. One of the greatest things in life is the awakening of our minds through change. I had mostly viewed change as negative, but I needed to start understanding change as positive. If I was to adapt to change, I needed to be amiable. To be amiable I needed to understand how to open my mind and adapt to each situation in front of me. I grew and learned when I was aware, through being amiable.

We walked for what seemed hours, but in reality it was just so damn cold. The winter that year was always slapping you in the face as soon as you walked outside. The three of us walked in a row across the field. My friend's brother led the way and he was walking quite fast. My head was down and I was breathing fast and shallow. I had that deep cold feeling, like there was just no way to get warm by moving, only by getting home and having a hot shower. It was quiet outside and amongst the rare sounds were our feet hitting the snow on the ground. We didn't speak until we stopped at a frozen river. There it was: our great debate, about thirty feet wide and the length of eternity. "Let's cross; we'll be fine," my friend's brother said. "Sure," I replied. We slowly began crossing the river, in a line again for some reason. All I heard was the sound of ice breaking and in an instant we were in the water. I was somehow out in front of the other two and I started to smash the ice and work my way toward land. I never looked behind me so I didn't know if the other two were following, but I hoped. I climbed up out of the water and reached for my friend. His brother was already on land. I pulled my friend out of the icy water. My hands were cold and bloodied from the ice. I had scrapes and cuts on my face too from hitting the ice on the way through. On our way home my feet felt hard pain, more and more with each step. It was like the cold water had frozen my feet with fire. Once we arrived back home we did what we needed to get warm with food, blankets, and hot showers. We were very quiet the remainder of the night. What a change I experienced that day. I adapted, and I was amiable in order to survive.

When certain events occurred at an early age, I always questioned why. Were they happening to test me? Did they happen because I needed to be shown and reminded that I was merely mortal? Did they happen so that I could define my thoughts, reflect, and adjust? To tell me I could be dead at any moment? Or maybe I was just over-thinking. But I wanted to test the boundaries. I needed to push the status quo and understand that my own unique ways were alright to live with. I knew there was more out there for me. I always reflected on what happened in my life, with thought, criticism, and compassion. I knew it was change I was now after.

Sometimes I would get too confident. Well, a lot of times I would get too confident. I was physically strong for my age, and fearless. I would do just about anything. I always thought I could do something until I realized you needed to practice first. The doubt never came to me until I was older. Ride a bike on just the front wheel? No problem; just let me eat the gravel road along the way. Get some extra help from friends to go down a zip line as fast as I could? Sure, let me lay in bed with a concussion for a week after. I thought I could run the fastest, jump the highest, and that a bullet couldn't stop me. In my mind the obstacles were never too hard or too dangerous. I was not someone who always pondered; I just did it. Perhaps it was my youthful brain doing a juggling act with consequences and rewards. As a kid, I was reckless at times. I would catch snakes by the dozen, was bitten by many of them, then I'd smash them with oars. I would throw rocks at frogs and birds because I thought I was hunting them. I would throw objects at trains and vandalize vacant property. It grew boring after a while though, and I resorted back to my shy, closed-in self. I soon learned I needed to be smart and calculate the risks, or I would be hurt in the process. Later in life I developed more resistance to new things that could potentially hurt me. I realized that living outside the norm didn't have to entail being a hoodlum. In order to rebel, I needed to have an amiable approach to the life I wanted, through intelligence, physical presence, and peace of mind. I would be myself and only be myself and that was true rebellion, because I refused to be anyone else but me. It's unfortunate that society asks a person to change into someone they aren't. I always felt as though the conveyer belt of society was only a guide, and I wanted to step outside it every so often.

I realized that being amiable could lead to self awareness and growth. Being amiable could mean adapting to situations, letting my guard down, being aware of my surroundings, and going with what unfolded in front of me naturally. People work really hard to be serious, when in reality I always felt life was too short to be taken seriously. To me, people who were so serious every minute of the day were creating walls. They had blinders on. They seemed closed off. Maybe this is my stubbornness, or my grandfather's will, but I refused to take life so seriously. If I did, I would've had a heart attack nine times over. In order to be amiable, we also need compassion and awareness. I started to link together these building blocks because they made sense to me. I became compassionate toward those who hurt me, and for some reason it was alright that they did, because I understood that they were human and they hadn't yet connected deeply with their souls. They weren't yet aware. I was amiable in the moment, and understood enough to rise above those moments.

It was my birthday, 9:11 in the morning. The day was peaceful yet exciting. My mind was focused on me, and my intentions that morning were to collect presents. "Zechariah, happy birthday!" my mother said excitedly as she opened my bedroom door. Our family tradition was to burst into each other's rooms with birthday presents and cheers. Sometimes I would pretend I was sleeping so that I wouldn't show my excitement. That morning my face lit up with a smile and I tried to hide it as best I could. For some reason as I grew older, I was embarrassed to show excitement. I guess I replaced excitement with fear, or maybe I thought that excitement showed weakness. I started to feel vulnerable if I showed excitement. After I opened my presents, we went into the kitchen to eat breakfast. The day was special because my mother made it special. The day was to be mine from breakfast through dinner until the time I went to bed. As bedtime approached, I could sense the household tense up. It was my mother and stepfather who were creating the tension. There had been subtle arguments throughout the day which I had paused briefly to observe. I seemed to observe these moments as if I was watching through a window. As parents, I felt they didn't connect to the idea that I was completely aware of what was happening around me, in our household. As I climbed into bed, my mother by my side, I smiled up at her. "Thank you Mom," I said. She leaned in and kissed me on the head, "You are welcome Zechariah, happy birthday. Goodnight." "Mom," I said. "Yes?" she asked. "Please don't yell tonight," I finally said. She looked at me, let out a big sigh, and shut the door. Though I was soon asleep I awoke to a loud noise. I wasn't sure what it was but it woke me up. I sat up in my bed and listened nervously. Shortly after, the screaming began. My mind changed from enjoying a day filled with love to enduring a night filled with terror. I adjusted and prepared myself for the worst as I had always done previously. I was amiable in my thoughts. I was amiable in my actions. It was a constant turn from one life to the next in only minutes. I often wondered if there was any break from the life that coexisted with my other life. I wished there was a break from being amiable in horrible situations. I wished there was a break from being an actor outside of the chaos.

I understood that when I accepted change, I could become amiable in the process. Every single situation in life is different, even if it may appear to be the same. The world is not black and white, but very colourful. I had to adapt to each situation and event through choosing my attitude.

When I was able to choose my attitude, and see things the way they were in front of me, rather than define the situation based on who I was, that is when I truly became in tune with the world, through being amiable.

1989

Strength

There is something refreshing about the nature of children. Children are enlightened by innocence and they carry a strength that never rests. I remember smiles as a child. I would smile all the time. When I meet children today, they are smiling. Obviously they smile because they have their own minds, their own opinions, and above all their own wills to accept the value of life for what it is. They are able to see the beauty in the moment. Children to me are like pure souls not yet touched by society. Their faces are fresh and full of light. Their existence happens to be so pure and real. They have strength because they are themselves and in themselves; they believe.

I woke up to glass smashing and a screeching yell that seemed to vibrate the house. I lay petrified and numb. My eyes were focused on one spot in the darkness and my heart was having ideas of its own, sending loud echoes throughout my body. As the vibrations grew louder, my mother's voice overtook the thoughts in my head. "Stop it! No! No! No! Get out!" she said. My younger sister was crying in her room, and my older sister stood in her room's doorway. My bedroom door opened and he came at me. He grabbed my arms firmly and said, "You are the man of the house, Zechariah; it's your job to take care of it." His eyes half closed and glazed over, his vest was old, brown, and weathered and his breath had that familiar odour. I heard the front door slam. I looked out my bedroom window and saw my younger sister draped over my stepfather's shoulder, bouncing up and down while he ran across the front lawn. I called the police. I spent the next two hours or so drawing at my desk because my mind needed to be distracted. I drew a dragon breathing fire at a knight in armour. The two officers came into my room. "I like your drawing," the first officer said. I looked up at him and gave a half smile. "Do you draw those often?" he asked. "I draw a lot, usually not dragons though," I remarked. "Do you draw often when these kinds of things happen?" he asked again while kneeling down next to me. "That's my bad-day pile," I responded, pointing to the stack of drawings on my desk. "All those pictures you drew are from days like today?" he asked. I nodded my head. "Yes." The other officer looked at me and said, "You've done a wonderful job, drawing these pictures." The next morning was like nothing had happened. He had spent the night in jail after smashing out the basement window and physically shattering my mother. I remember looking at him when he got home and searching for peace. In his fast paced walk by me, he apologized quickly, and then went to the basement. My mother lay in bed, sleeping most of the day with her arms outstretched and bruised. I knew for certain these events didn't belong in our lives. They had to stop.

My mother seemed distant, but never acknowledged this. "Mom, are you alright?" I asked. She looked at me with a blank stare and replied, "What do you want to do today, Zechariah?"

"I just want to draw, Mom, what should I draw?" My mother looked at me with a puzzled look, clearly thinking through her response and trying to find the words that would otherwise be simple to speak. "Draw a horse or a boat," she said softly. "Mom, you always want me to draw weird things," I said with a twisted look on my face. "Well I guess I am weird then," she responded. Her soul was detached when I talked to her. Her strength was vacant. A tornado of emotional and physical torment that would last for years was defining who I was, and who I would become. Hell, it was defining all of us, my mother and two sisters included. How does one overcome this environment? What would we know differently when we got older, and how would I stop it from happening again? These are questions I would carry for years. I pondered about life, friends, adults, parents, and the potential of a happy existence that wasn't as far fetched as I thought. Most importantly, I wondered what was out there for me, as opposed to the concrete walls of torment I had been surrounded by for what seemed like an eternity already. How could I possibly look at the world in a positive light, growing up in these conditions? How could I look at the world through the eyes of peace and trust, when everything I knew was the opposite? How could I continue to find the strength?

It was 3:09 in the afternoon on a Tuesday in the month of April when my mother didn't get out of bed. I wondered if she was sick. I knocked on her door and heard her answer, "What?" I asked if I could come in, and when I got no response I opened the door anyway. A smell of sweat wrapped around my face, and I proceeded to walk slowly toward the bed. She was laying in the dark, looking through the wall at nothing. "Mom?" I asked quietly. No reply. "Mom!" I said a bit louder. No reply. I walked out of the room and shut the door behind me. I had homework to do, but who really cared? The next day I awoke and my mother was already up, encouraging me to get out of bed for school. It was confusing for me. I remember thinking she was some sort of stranger, but I didn't argue. My mother had somehow found a trace of strength again. I knew my mother would always find her strength, but when you are beaten down so many times, the strength weakens more and more until there is none left.

It was inner strength that helped me recognize that I would overcome. I would make the choice to move on because I knew I had the strength. Sometimes I would move forward without even understanding how. When I stood strong both mentally and physically, I found out who I really was. Strength was my soul's ability to push on in life. Strength was something deep inside my mind that carried me through life. Strength was something deep inside my mind that carried me through life. Although I always believed there may have been some unexplainable source of my strength, strength would ultimately be my own creation.

1990

Overcome

I never feared strangers like I feared other things in my life. I never feared letting them into my life and I never feared giving to them or caring for them. I later found out we can learn a lot from strangers because they hold answers to questions we didn't realize we had. I got on a bus once and a young boy was staring at me with a strange look on his face. He was clearly thinking about something. I smiled at him and he asked me, "Where are you heading?" I paused briefly. "Nowhere special," I replied. He then said that the bus was taking him to see his father. I looked back at him and said, "Then that's a very important trip." He looked at me and said, "I am scared because I haven't seen him in many years." "Well, maybe you should be excited then," I responded. He looked back at me and smiled, saying, "I know I will overcome my fear once I see him." I smiled back and sat in my seat. I realized that to overcome in life, you need to face life directly.

It was 2:09 on a Saturday morning and I heard my mother and stepfather arguing. By this time it was routine. I would wake up and listen as though my life depended on it, most times frozen from fear. All I could hear was my breathing in the dead silence, waiting for the eruption. As I lay in the bed listening, I could feel the urge to get involved, to keep stepping in so maybe one day it would end. I slowly got out of bed, my heart pounding, my throat dry, and my mouth open, breathing heavily. I stood at the doorway and pressed my head against it. And then stupidly I decided to wander out into the living room and ask, "Why are you yelling at each other? Why do you keep doing this?" I stood in front of him, he said nothing, and then he reached out. He grabbed me, squeezing my arms, and my face curled up like I'd just eaten a raw onion. Some weird noises came from me, kind of like a whimper as though I'd been punched in the stomach. With all his force, he threw me onto a coffee table that was littered with drinking glasses from the night before. I slid across the surface and then there was silence. I lay on the table: scared, confused, and alone. In the hospital it was chaotic. First the glass was pulled from my face and skull, and as the stitches were embedded in my head, the pain grew worse. My soul felt squeezed and broken. For many days after, I remained in my room.

I was sad, defeated, confused, and tired. With that incident, pain began to lead me to another area in my life. It was too painful to fight, too painful to react. The pain seeped through me and I regurgitated nothing but sadness. I had only the remains of the violence lingering in my soul. I continued to pursue an understanding of it all, searching deep within my mind, searching within my heart. Searching for answers I never knew how to find. Questions floated around me. What would happen to me next? What would happen to my family? How could it be like this? How could I keep finding myself surrounded by chaos, pain, and these volatile creatures? What did I do to make this happen? My parents had become creatures to me. I saw them as dark and soulless, walking around without reason. They continued to fight, screaming, punching, kicking and grasping at life through the demons that taunted them. Angry and distraught, I knew most parents were not like this. I looked into their eyes and saw nothing. I felt their presence around me, but felt nothing. It was vacant.

Within weeks of school starting, more events unfolded. One night I mouthed back at the alcoholic rage that was my stepfather, "Come on tough guy, think you're so awesome?" I was grabbed, and my back was rammed into a wall. My spine stopped at the wood stud inside the wall and I looked up and said, "You're fixing that!" as I pulled myself out of the mess. I felt the pain and ache through my body linger for some time. My face met the floor on an ongoing basis. I skidded across the carpet, tile, and linoleum on the floors in the house, but tried my best not to show the pain and anger created inside me. My anger was suppressed in order to never prove weakness and to show that I would never back down. My body, youthful in its structure, felt aged in its existence. I felt like a mistreated prisoner in the very home that was supposed to be full of safety, trust, and love. My nights were filled with tears, and my thoughts were paralyzed by the very possibility of the fear to come, only to hide all of it each day from the outside world as if I was wearing a mask. To be around my stepfather was like being around someone who was only angry at me for something I knew nothing of. It was like walking around a minefield: confused where to step, what to say, and what to do. Make the wrong move and shit blew up. I didn't know this person in the slightest anymore, or even understand completely what was going on. I was only trying to live my life as a child.

I came home one day to find my room packed. My mother sat down beside me on my bed. "You are going to live with your father," she said quietly. I looked up at her and quickly responded, "Sure." I didn't ask why, because I was so confused. I thought maybe it was better this way so I didn't want to argue it. I just wasn't sure what prompted her decision. My mother gave no explanation and I took it to heart, feeling as though it was something I had done.

A few days later I walked into my new school with my father, and I noticed that the hallways were much larger but darker compared to my old school. We headed to the principal's office to register. "What grades do you usually get, Zechariah?" the principal asked. "Usually A's," I said shyly. As I was shown where my first period class was, I placed my stuff inside my assigned locker and then opened the door to the classroom. I was a bit nervous and of course, angry. Silence was strong until my friend blurted my name and the class resumed. Fortunately I had previously known this kid from taking art classes together during the summer when I would stay with my father. I would walk to school with him because we lived near one another. One winter morning, as we were crossing a bridge over the highway, he walked on the outside of the railing. "What are you doing; it's snowing like crazy, be careful!" I yelled at him. "Calm down man, I'm fine," he yelled back. I looked down at him halfway across the bridge and noticed that his balance was off. He stumbled and then slid down the rest of the way. His body hit the edge and his hands caught on. There he was, hanging over the edge with a twenty foot drop below. I carefully made my way down and grabbed his arms. "Hang on, hang on. Grab my hands, man!" I yelled. "Holy shit, grab my hands!" I yelled again. For some reason we both started laughing. It made us weak in the moment but we quickly went straight faced as I lifted him up, then we laughed hysterically again while laying on the edge. We got up and kept walking to school without hesitation. Shit like that happened a lot when I was young.

After class one day I was exchanging books at my locker when a young girl approached me with her friends standing close behind. "Can I have your number?" she asked. I froze and looked at the girl. I got scared, was thrown off, and could only think of one word. "No," I responded shyly. A few nights later, our phone rang and my stepmother answered. "Hello? Just a minute; Zechariah, the phone is for you," she said as she put the phone down on the table. "Hello?" I said. "Is this Zechariah?" a girl's voice said. "Yes," I responded. There was a long pause and I could hear people talking in the background. "Asshole!" they all shouted at once before hanging up. I pretended to keep talking, "Sure, sounds good, see you tomorrow," and then placed the phone down. I walked past my father and stepmother and made my way to my room. I stood at the window, staring out at the yard, and began to cry. A few weeks later I signed up for a martial arts class. My first experience was a test of some kind of kata and some moves my sensei taught me. The next class, I had to repeat the moves. As I repeated what I learned, my sensei observed closely and placed me into an adult class. It was my escape and energy source at the time. Martial arts to me were important; they carved out my first spiritual connection with my mind and body. Though I had always made friends easily, and attended a number of new schools, this time was different. I could feel myself closing off to a lot of my surroundings, so I needed martial arts more than anything else. I needed to escape the ridiculous behaviour of people around me and have some sort of structure to help me overcome.

It was 9:29 on a Tuesday night and I sat on the couch watching my father and stepmother talk, argue, and co-exist. I sat in silence and watched. I felt like I was not even there as my mind wandered into other areas of my life. I walked out of the room and there I was, alone in my existence. If they didn't know I was there, who would ever really know I existed? I thought I needed to fix it all and I thought I needed to change who I was. I didn't want to be there and I didn't want to be back at home with my mother. Who wanted me? School was just something to get me out of the house, but I didn't want to be there either. My grades slipped, my fears grew, and I lashed out again. I vandalized and broke into a school close by, only to steal a fax machine I couldn't do anything with. I skipped school and wanted nothing to do with anyone who would put order into my life.

By the time summer came around, I was just going through the motions. One weekend my aunt and uncle came to visit. Me, my father, and my uncle decided to go go-karting. As we were leaving, I remember my father being asked by my uncle if he was okay to drive. "I'm fine," he replied. This confused me because I didn't exactly know what he meant by that question. We drove separately in my father's car, and my uncle drove in his own car. On the way my dad cut some guy off and he smashed on his horn. Dad was pissed off and started to yell back at him. "Fuck you, you stupid asshole!" gesturing with his hands. I felt rather embarrassed and slouched down in the seat. As we arrived at the track I could see how fast the karts really were. It was exciting. Now, these weren't your typical go-karts. People had died on this track and we were required to sign waivers. We grabbed helmets, paid, and signed our lives away. The three of us took to the track, me getting a head start and ripping off as fast as I could. My father attempted to pass me and take over first place. As we neared a corner halfway around the track, his tire hit mine, and off I went. The kart rolled, skidded across the track, and came to a stop partially on the grass through the tire barrier. I climbed out of the kart, stood up, and glanced back. The steering wheel and frame were bent, and one tire was completely ripped off. I looked down at myself. The blood dripping from my knee and arm was at a constant flow. One of the workers came over and started to freak out on me, "Look at the fuck'n' kart, man, the steering wheel is fucked." "I'm fine," I said, before he possibly took the time to ask. My uncle came running over, asked if I was okay, and then gave my father a funny look. When my father asked if we could continue, the guy who worked on the track said only one of us could go back out there. I never said a word but without hesitation my father said, "He cut me off. I'm going back out there." As I walked back to the office, helmet in hand, my idea of fun changed and I became angry. The drive home was quiet. I wondered why he had done that. I wondered why he was so eager to not give notice to my condition, and get back out there. When I walked back into the house I noticed the beer bottles on the kitchen counter. I had to overcome what happened that day and I had to bite my tongue. I knew it was not my father I had spent the day with. It was the alcohol.

I decided to take the train back to my mother's when school was let out. I knew I would not return to my father's. All I had with me were my comic books and the clothes that I was wearing. My attitude was to sit alone and hope to not talk to anyone. Quiet was ideal for me, as I was growing distant and becoming a recluse from the world. I was still young but I was always wondering about life and what it was about. Why it was the way it was. My thought processes at this age took me places I didn't think possible. But as life put me in certain situations, I began understanding from a larger perspective. I was becoming a deep thinker. "Great, the train is fucking packed," I mumbled to myself. Here I was, searching for a seat, and the only seat left was beside an elderly lady. I asked if I could sit down beside her, and she responded, "Of course you can." I said hello and sat down. As the trip progressed, she tried to talk to me, and I tried to avoid talking to her. If she had been someone who was turned off by rudeness, she would have turned the other way and shut her mouth. But this woman kept talking. I finally gave in and listened to her stories about her travels, her family, and her kids. Her children were grown up by now with children of their own. Silence stirred for a while until she turned to me and politely commented, "You know, I grew up in a very traumatic environment similar to you." This confused me. How did she know what was going on in my life? I was speechless, and there was silence. She continued on about how each of our lives is not something that was given to us by fate, but given to us through a learning process that enabled fate to take place. "There is a lesson that someone wants you to understand and the understanding will help you overcome," she explained. She continued to tell me that lessons in life are a gift but only if we choose to see them, both the hard ones and the easy ones. She explained to me what anger was and that it was important to curb it early, because to alter such behaviour too late in life would hold me back. She talked about forgiveness and sorrow. She talked about how we cannot change people; they have to find the light themselves, but maybe we can give them a gentle push at times. "Allow yourself to grow and you will see the other side. The life bulb will continue to shine brighter and you will see things more clearly," she said forcefully. My thoughts raced as she talked, and I even once wondered if I was talking to an empty seat.

The lady on the train had eyes that were pure. Eyes, after all, are windows to the purity of one's soul. Purity can sometimes diminish, depending on the damage we experience in our lifetime. It can also diminish depending on damage that is self-induced, or damage which is brought upon us without asking. Our eyes can depict who we are, honest or not, kind or not, and they tell our story. The woman on the train looked into my eyes deeply when she talked to me. She understood and felt who I was without even knowing me. People are more perceptive then I give them credit for. People are good and people do care. Strangers care. I also learned once again that there is always worse in the world, and maybe I didn't have it too bad. The self pity was dissipating and I would learn to curb my anger. Before the woman got off the train at her stop, I gently touched her arm, thanked her, and smiled. "You will overcome," she whispered in her calming voice. Her words would echo through me forever.

I was realizing that these people I met in my life left something with me. They helped me overcome in some way. By overcoming I found peace, and strength, and was able to reach a place in my life where I could move forward and keep pushing. Was I afraid? I always feared things in my life. I knew that I needed to respect challenges rather than fear them. If I was afraid, I would paralyze myself. I felt that to truly understand myself, I first needed to understand others, accept others, and allow others to reach out to me.

Overcome. This was an important word that I chose along the way. I continued to understand that overcoming was one of those things I was searching for. It became engrained within me. It was what I always felt deep inside. I always knew I would overcome, and if I was to overcome, I would succeed.

1991

Truth

A young boy sat silently on the road outside the house. I asked him what he was up to. "I fell and hurt my leg," he answered. I asked how he fell. "I am going to be in a race at school. I fell running." "Very cool, so keep going then." He looked at me, nodded his head, stood up and said, "I was thinking I couldn't do it because it hurt so badly, but I know I can push beyond the pain and keep going." Everything has a surface, but we find the meaning deep down. Our lives are mostly on the surface. But when we dig deep into the reality, we find some pain, but we also find some truth. It's a shame when we spend all our time only pushing through difficulties on the surface. Through constant reflection, what matters most is how we adapt, learn, grow, and finally understand the depth of the meaning. And in the end, truth remains through what seemed impossible.

Life is blurry at times. It's hard to see the truth. It's hard to focus. This I had always known.

When I searched for truth, I searched for meaning along the way. My truth was defined through a series of facts or events through living in a pure, untwisted, non-manipulated mentality away from what I knew. It was vital to define it this way. I believed that truth comes in all shapes and sizes; however, the truth could be difficult to uncover, like unmasking a path to happiness. The more I understood the truth, and accepted the truth, the happier I became. 1991 was full of truths that defined me and my purpose at that time. I realized humans can be horrible, selfish, spiteful, and jealous. Humans can be vindictive and malicious in ways I never thought possible. Humans can be deceitful, dishonest, and hurtful. Humans can be gross. I also realized that humans have such a strong capacity to do wonderful things in life. Were we real with ourselves through honesty and truth? Did honesty lead to trust? I would create distance with others before they created distance with me because trust was hard to understand in my life. However, I realized that through trust came truth and through truth came trust.

2:09 in the afternoon on a Monday and it was recess. I grabbed onto the zip line out in the yard that was suspended about ten feet off the ground, closing my fists tightly around the bar. Two friends grabbed my legs and ran with me full force. They let go, and I zipped down the line with fierce velocity, or at least what I thought was fierce at the time. A tire at the end of the line offered a softening stop; however, for some reason I found my own way to stop. The bar hit the tire and my body swayed forward, feet up in the air with continued momentum. I let go. I saw blue, then black. I watched the grass beneath me pass by my feet as I was being helped back inside the school, and into the classroom. I sat at my desk and focused on the wall without thoughts. My teacher turned his head, looked at me strangely, and finally spoke, "Zechariah, are you alright?" Some of the kids responded for me,

"He fell outside!" I made a trip to the hospital, and spent a week in bed with a severe concussion. Did that fall change me? Did it affect who I am, who I was going to be? It's the simple things in our lives that possibly make the largest difference. Could intuition have prevented it? Gut feelings? A sixth sense? Can any of these things protect us? Did they lead me to truth? I knew that physical pain brought truth; that was for sure.

That summer I continued to play baseball. Although I was okay at it, it was never a passion in my life. I was a pitcher in a windmill league but found it too boring, and stopped playing once I was in high school. I was winning art contests locally and outside my area, though in that moment I thought nothing of it. One of my paintings was selected to go into a local hospital, and was shown in an auditorium in front of an audience. The host asked what was in my thoughts while I was painting the piece. "Maybe Zechariah will let us know what was on his mind when he painted this," he said to the audience. I didn't have a response at that time; however, I thought about it later. The painting was of rocks - different shapes and sizes, various colours and tones. The rocks were sharp, strong, and solid in their appearance. In the middle was a small, gentle waterfall, guiding a stream of water through the ever changing environment of the world. The painting depicted my journey through the different stages of life, the highs and lows, the rough patches and the quiet serene times. The water was moving on a journey that would unfold only in the moment through the space provided. The water jumped off its highest point, meeting the bottom with a thunderous crash, to find chaos, turmoil, and punishment. However, when the fall was done, the truth of the journey was realized.

I realized that truth in my life was laid out in front of me. I saw truth in my family, and also truth in the events that surrounded us. When I accepted my family for who they were, I accepted truth. But I also understood that deep down a lot of the chaos was not truly them. They were something more; they were human, compassionate and alive, in pain and lost. Truth to me was being real with myself rather than living with a mask on, and I needed someone or something to remove that mask. That was the real challenge. I had to accept things that were really part of me and my life in order to be truthful. I became more anxiety ridden. I could feel it eat at me through the anticipation of bad things to come. I could feel it because I was on a mission to discover truth. I needed to combat this now because I had figured out its strong potential to come out at a later age. I had to think about the long term effects on the family of my own I would have one day: children, wife, and friends. I knew the reality was that I had to face this head-on; otherwise, I would be held captive my entire life. How long this would take, I would never know. I had to be true; however, could I be truthful with others?

When truth is constant, trust grows. I learned to trust myself and trust who I was, because I lived in truth. Because of the events in my life it was hard to trust my parents, and in turn it was hard to trust others. Though I would continue to struggle in trusting others, I knew that I eventually had to in order to have successful relationships. I made a pact with myself: I would always do my best to live my life in truth.

1992

Friends

There was that kid again…staring at me from the curb of the road as I sat on my front steps. "What's your question today?" I asked. The kid replied with a smile, "Where are your friends?" "They are right here," I replied, pointing to my heart.

It was autumn, my favourite season of the year. I began high school. I had a couple of friends from public school, but that group was about to grow. Here I was on my lunch break with my public school friend, walking closely behind two others who were also friends with each other from public school. My friend knew the others in front of us, so he quickly jogged up to them. I followed. "Get out of here, you aren't part of this group!" soon followed. I didn't say anything but just kept walking, somewhat trailing the group of three. It only took three months until that same kid who had told me to leave turned into my best friend. We were matched in gym class. We were the same weight so we had to wrestle against each other. Although I can't remember who won that day, I know we both won overall. We remain friends to this very day, and will continue to be friends until the day we die.

As much as I acted like I didn't care if I fit in or not, when I was young I always wanted to fit in. Most times I was always scared people would find out what was going on at home, but for some reason with my friends this never crossed my mind. The fact that I felt safe said a lot to me about them as people. As I got older, my attitude changed and I figured if someone didn't like me, then that was fine, life goes on. I usually did this by keeping quiet and observing for a while to get a better understanding of who I was surrounded by. At times people would take that as something negative and turn my quietness or distance against me. My trust was difficult to keep, but not difficult to earn.

Who knew that a bond between friends could systematically alter life's direction? I continued to be scared to make new friends for only one reason, and that was bringing them to my house. But I knew having friends could provide stability in a life where an unknown path and a broken foundation led the way. I knew and understood the importance of friends. My friends were different; they were special, and part of who I was. One thing I was always able to do was choose good people in my life. That never changed. It was like I secretly selected each friend to be a mentor in my life. Each of them would offer their own unique blend of insight and strength to my world. How rare it is to have such good friends. High school brought many friends, and it all unfolded relatively effortlessly. Was it meant to be? Friends would have the largest impact in my life, and thankfully they guided me toward good. To be loved and love is something remarkably precious. Who knew this would come from a group of high school friends. The best way to bond with someone, whether with friends, family, or partners, is to let them be who they are and let the relationship unfold naturally. My friends did this. Their acceptance and patience created a tremendous bond of trust. I began to believe that relationships are vital to help find our purpose. Friends offer guidance, trust, support, values, morals, ethics, health, and happiness. I truly believe that without my friends I would have gone a different direction in my life.

My friends were different. They were special, and were a part of who I was. Each friend offered their own unique blend of insight and strength in my world, silently through their actions, and at times, their words. They opened their arms to people and the events that transpired in front of them. We laughed all the time, and sometimes we even cried in front of each other. I would find myself beginning to observe life rather than participate, especially in high school. I watched as people interacted, showed love, hate, compassion, talked about others behind their backs, cried, fought, and yelled. I always reflected on my observations and continued to correct myself so that I would not look so foolish or vulnerable. I took notice especially around my friends' parents. They communicated in ways that were so different from what I knew or understood. They respected each other, they were at peace, and there was no violence about to erupt at a moment's notice. I enjoyed staying over at my friends' places because I slept well. I slept in peace.

A friend and I were sitting out on the boardwalk in town, beside the river when I finally opened up. "My family's a mess," I said, out of nowhere. He looked at me and smiled. "Shit, we're all messed in some way," he said back. "No, I mean things are going on that just aren't right. My stepdad is beating the shit out of my mom and he drinks heavily, drinks daily, and I don't know how to stop it," I spoke directly. My friend paused, and looked at me with his eyes wider than before. "You ever get hit?" he asked.

I showed him a couple of scars. "Wow, man, I am sure you can stay with us if you really need to. My mom would take you in, no hesitation," my friend said as he put his arm around me. "Also, just so you know, it doesn't change who you are to me. You will always be important in my life," he added, with a serious look on his face. I smiled, nodded my head, and felt like I had just won the lottery.

Success. Who was to define this word for me? I was. I would base my success on life experience, friends, growth, and happiness. My friends accepted who I was, always. Regardless of the things around me, the car I drove or house I lived in, success would not be complete without friends, internal happiness, love, and health. I always thought that in life, one should celebrate more. My friends gave me that opportunity. Every little achievement in our lives was due for a celebration. My friends helped me understand what success was, and in turn, I understood what friends were to me. My sense of appreciation grew through my friends. I knew I had many friends because I was myself a friend to many. I tuned into what really mattered most. Through my friends, I learned how to give more than take, and understood that it was that idea which brought me happiness. I learned how to build character and trust through my friends. It was easy to be there for my friends before I was there for myself. They all deserved it.

"Even though we've changed and we're all finding our own place in the world, we all know that when the tears fall or the smile spreads across our face, we'll come to each other because no matter where this crazy world takes us, nothing will ever change so much to the point where we're not all still friends." This quotation resonated with me, though I never knew who said it. I decided to write my own thoughts on friendship:

In years to come
In our lives to live,
We remain strong
We remain one,

Together we travel
As a group we grow,
A bond forever
Our strength we show,

Let us be what we are
Let us shine as friends,
Our trust and power
Has no end

I was lying in bed at midday, around 12:09 in the afternoon, and my thoughts were bouncing off the walls. My ideas were scattered. Music from Pearl Jam playing in the background was my only voice. I felt like I was floating out at sea, slowly moving side to side, up and down, rhythmically in awareness. I was numb, saddened, and alone. I then heard footsteps running up the stairs and quickly sat up. My door opened faster than I could blink and they came tumbling in. I was relieved to see it was my friends. "Zechariah!" my friends yelled. "What are you doing here, guys?" I asked. "Grab your stuff, we're heading out to play some ball then grab something to eat. Get off your lazy ass and let's go," my friend said. "Alright, alright, hold on," I answered, laughing. As we walked downstairs, one friend put his arm around me and quietly asked, "You okay, man?" I looked at him and nodded. We all piled in the car, and I sat in the backseat, thinking, smiling, and reminding myself that all of this was awesome. After all, I wasn't alone anymore.

I could never completely explain my friendships to others. It was more the feelings that resonated through each of us that we just knew were there. Our acceptance of one another was astounding. I have a thousand stories I could tell about my friends. We spent most of our time laughing. We laughed so hard we cried. My friends have filled a lifetime of memories. I treasure the words from each of them that have always been a part of our relationships: "Hey man, whatever you need."

T.S. Eliot said, "We shall not cease from exploration, and the end of all our exploring will be to arrive where we started and know the place for the first time." I always felt that no matter what I had, if I had my friends nothing else could compare. Why would I ever want more, when everything I needed was right in front of me? When I wondered how much I really meant in the world, I decided that the answer was in my friends. I would love them all more than they would ever know.

My friends saved me.

1993

Growth

I sat on my front lawn, looking at the broken down house in the field across the gravel road. A kid, riding by on a bicycle, stopped when our eyes met. He asked, "What are you up to?" I replied hesitantly, because I didn't really know. "Looking at that house." He asked me why I was looking at the house, and I responded, "Not really sure." His last comment before he rode off got me thinking: "Looks like it could use some nurturing and care. I would think it can be saved." I watched as he rode off faster than he appeared and thought about the growth potential if this house was given some attention and nurturing. Growth was something I could help create.

I arrived home from basketball practice and went straight to the kitchen. Dinner lay on a plate wrapped in aluminum foil in the fridge. I heated up the food and finished off the rest of the milk. Twenty minutes later I heard rumbling, "Who drank the fucking milk?!" The fridge door slammed shut and I heard a chair being pushed into the table. My mother went downstairs to quiet him down but he went off. I locked my door and hoped he wouldn't come into my room, although at this point I was ready for him. I stood near the door with my fist cocked back ready to swing if he came in. He went straight to his bedroom and slammed the door. For the next two years I ate in my room every night and didn't drink any milk. I also became acutely aware of what my body did before violence would take place. The sensations that would arise were very real and the fear that would course through my bones resembled that of a cold winter's wind. My eyes became intense, staring into the darkness, my body was motionless, my sense of hearing grew heightened, and my breathing became slowed in a controlled angry pattern. I could feel my blood flowing through me, powerful, like I was a bath tub of water being tilted back and forth. My mind was frozen from thoughts, and the only thing left was my slowly thawing anger. For me it was a moment of survival. For the predator, it was alcoholic rage.

I was an empty shell. I doubted myself and my capabilities. I felt like a cracked carcass carrying around my guts, spilling my confidence all over the place. It seemed like I was there, but actually I was nowhere. You could see me but I wasn't present. I was disappearing. I started to really understand the survival techniques, and I understood how to make it through every night. I understood how to wear a mask at school, around my friends, and out in public, while pretending that everything was just normal. I understood the dangers at home, which by now had become second nature. Living in fear was wearing me down; whether I knew this or not, I would eventually see the results. By this age I would show signs of wear, both mental and physical, like I had expired and only my body remained. I was beat. I was exhausted, and each day it was hard to find enough energy to push forward. Guidance to me was understated and vacant. I would eat alone in my room every night. I was surrounded by my thoughts, passions, and wants, but I didn't know how to attain them, nor did I understand that I could. Most times we were so poor that we had to choose between food on the table or a phone line. We would endure money problems and loss of homes. Loss was something I began to grow accustomed to.

When I wasn't with my friends, music was my only solace. The lyrics would resonate through the anger that kept building. I became trapped in a paradox, viewing life only from the outside. I observed life but didn't engage. I became completely distant from the life that was going on in front of me. Even though I had fought so hard to get this far, I was running out of gas, and I was at a loss.

I began to think of my confidence and question where it was. It seemed to me that confidence comes when the mind is confined to one thought process. To be confident is sometimes to not know better. Knowing less can sometimes prevent failure from creeping in, because we stick to our initial thought. Ignorance can play a key role in life, because it doesn't let us consider the possibility of failure. My mind would head in about thirty directions of thought over a simple idea. I would conjure up an idea and my mind would take off with multiple thoughts coming from out of nowhere. I would be bombarded first by the initial idea, and then that idea would morph into what I thought was a better idea. I would stew in the ideas, tormenting myself with better ones until my confidence in the initial idea was lost and the confusion was insurmountable. This thought cycle paralyzed me. This confusion sent me far away from confidence. The root of the problem was that I knew better, and this awareness made my confidence decline over time. At the end of my thoughts, when I considered the effects of my actions, it was always failure that took over. As much as I embraced failure, its inevitability scared me. I thought of the darkness. I thought too deeply at times, getting trapped in my own mind. Thinking was the sticky fly trap tape that I couldn't get away from. Sometimes I wished I was just a simple thinker, avoiding the depths of thought. I was mostly puzzled by trying to understand why I thought this way.

My thoughts collected like dust, rapidly and without warning. My thoughts formed into a rubber band, pulling my confidence with tense resistance. I wondered if my confidence had possibly been taken from me. But my thoughts needed to move forward, and I needed to get rid of the bitterness in order to create potential for growth. Buddhist monks believe that bitterness must be swallowed before one can move forward. I needed to get past the old stuff. Was I not allowing myself to grow? Was it my surroundings? At times I felt like everyone around me was growing, just not me. Who was I to blame? Although I was in my teens, I felt like I was still in my early childhood. It felt like time was frozen, because I was still dealing with the same things over and over again. I thought of my father's beer bottles; they brought bad things, not celebration. When could I begin to celebrate?

It was 3:09 on a Sunday afternoon and I was on the riding lawnmower cutting grass in the backyard. Our dog was chasing me as she always did, happy, and in retrospect, half retarded. But she loved us regardless. I always worried that the lawnmower would throw out a rock that would hit the dog, but it never did. I had my music plugged into my walkman, mixed tape inserted. The music put me in a trance state of mind and the hour flew by. As I parked the lawn mower in the shed, my mother came out. I turned my music down. "Thank you, Zechariah. Your friend called while you were cutting the grass." "We sure do cut the grass a lot, Mom," I replied. "It needs it, Zechariah, don't be lazy," she finally said. Naturally the grass would grow given the proper surroundings, the right amount of water, sun, and oxygen, which led me to think; I don't get why we can't just let things be what they naturally are. But then I thought that was just me being lazy, as my mother had said, and an excuse to get out of cutting the grass.

Growth was something I defined through intellectual maturation and development, along with life's events shaping and molding me into who I became. In 1993, first and foremost, the growth came from my friends. My mind evolved towards maturity in spite of my surroundings. I tried to understand my surroundings as much as I could, but it was only the presence of my friends who were able to bring perspective. My perspective was bounced around and grasped because of my friends' families. I eventually realized that I had reached awareness, and that I was growing in ways I didn't think were possible. I was beginning to understand the dynamics of my household, and the impact of the events on each family member.

I became more aware of people and their feelings, their thoughts, and their actions. I recognized that I was developing in ways that made me believe I deserved more, but this also brought the realization that I was trapped. I felt that I didn't deserve to just carry on through life, but to experience life. I deserved to really take life in through the good things available to me. I saw my life through a child's eyes, not as an adult, which would later be a detriment. I think I eventually disowned my family without them really knowing it. I was there, but not entirely part of a family unit. This needed to happen, but in the end I wish we had been more of a family. We were a family with nothing on the inside. The bad events in our family life overshadowed the good ones. There were traces of love, primarily through my mother, and I recognized this when it happened. I just wish I had acknowledged this more to my mother along the way.

I also became more aware of my words, the way I approached others, my emotions, the way I treated others, and the way my body language was perceived. I became aware of some flaws I had. I slowly became aware of my opportunities for improvement. I realized I needed to step aside from my ego to learn open-heartedly and grow as a person. Sometimes this would take me a while after an especially hard lesson, but I eventually made it through. I learned, reflected, and became stronger. This process lit my way so that I could perceive the lessons ahead.

It was a sunny afternoon and I sat along the water watching the leaves swim by. I looked down at my feet and then back up to the sky. I wondered about the changing world, the earth, and the elements. The world grows and sometimes humans hold it back. What confused me in my observations was that the earth seemed to be suppressed in growth, while I was allowed to grow freely. How could I prevent this from happening? This was hard to accept. I needed to connect to my opportunities and take nothing for granted. I needed to appreciate that growth was a choice. I could take advantage of it and that would be okay. I could see growth right in front of me, and it was extremely bright. Growth was my decision. Growth can be defined differently for each person. I like to think of it as the mind enabling fresh thoughts that can lead to a better life. Going through the events that were in front of me was my opportunity for growth.

I knew I was gaining clarity; I just needed to figure out how to fully understand and embrace growth.

1994

Passion

As I walked through the garden near the town hall, the young boy stood tall along the edge of the grass. He looked at me as I made my way toward him and smiled the entire time. He carried with him a small book and a pencil. I asked him, "What do you have there?" He looked down at the book and back at me. "I do sketches," he replied. I asked him why and he looked at me puzzled. "It's a sketch pad I keep because I like to draw. It's my passion!" he said excitedly. "Passion?" I asked. "Yes, passion. I love it and I'm going to be a great artist because of my passion," he finally said. I smiled and kept walking, but wondered what I was passionate about. I came up with a few ideas, and then I thought long and hard about the word passion. I decided that passion was living with a drive from within my soul about what I love in life.

I began playing basketball in grade eight, only to find I was horrible at it. Coming from my hockey and baseball background, this seemed like a weird sport to transition to. I was shooting hoops outside during recess once and a classmate laughed at me. She was a lot taller than me and also seemed to be much better than I was at basketball. I wanted to change that. For some reason, her laughter hit me hard. It grew on me and I felt a drive like no other to prove to her, and most importantly myself, that I could accomplish anything. I could never say never in life. To put limits on what we can achieve is unreasonable and unthinkable. So, I ate, drank, and lived basketball. I had a ball in my hands wherever I went. I played and lived basketball. I wanted to fly, like in my childhood dreams, and I wanted to be the best.

The best way I can explain what I felt when I played basketball was this: the ball in my hands was like an extension of my being, an elegant symphony of physical creativity. Every time I played, I could smell the leather of the ball mixed with sweat and exertion. I loved that smell. At times we would play on lowered rims so we could dunk. Getting a lead pass thrown to me, I knew I was about to take off. All of my hard practice and childhood dreams of flying unfolding into reality. I dribbled the ball to a point where I knew I could launch toward the rim. My legs bent, and then exploded off the ground, and for a moment I flew. My arms provided momentum as I exerted as much force as I could to float to the rim. My body hung in the air, away from all my troubles, time standing still, all pain and fear removed and released. As I came down, I slammed the ball as hard as I could with my arm extended. My hand grabbed the rim after the ball passed through. For a moment, I was a king. I felt invincible. It was beautiful and it lit a fire inside me. I knew that for the first time in my life I actually felt more love for something than I had ever thought possible. I could play for hours and not realize that the world had passed me by. I sensed that there was a distinct truth out on the basketball court. I couldn't fake my skills, fake a good shot, or fake my way through a game. I had a true passion for the sport.

I even played basketball in the snow, because nothing would hold me back. Passion is what drove me. I learned that life feels better when passion is involved. When I was passionate about something, the world became brighter, and I quickly evolved through time with purpose. I felt as if I could finally fly.

I was not an athlete, not a scholar, not a movie star or singer. I was me. I would soon celebrate the small things in my life because I discovered they carried momentum toward the larger successes. I had strong desires that transformed into dreams, but then back again to desires. I knew not of dreams because I had spent too long desiring something outside of the chaos. If no one around me was going to celebrate my life's victories, I would do this alone. I had to celebrate my achievements to help protect my passions and realize that my dreams were attainable. I needed to hold myself accountable to the energy I brought to life. Imagining that everything in this world holds a place of passion in someone's heart and soul brought a smile to my face. I knew that not everyone had a passion, but I always hoped they would eventually find it.

9:09 in the evening and I was back into the reality I knew. He was drinking. He turned and looked at me, confused because I was out of my room. He saw the mess in the kitchen and rifled a chair across the floor. We all went silent. His eyes were red and deep with pain and anger. His body was tense and robotic as he navigated himself around the house. He grabbed my mother and pushed her into the kitchen table while her feet skidded across the floor. She didn't say anything. I stood in the room beside the kitchen breathing heavily. My sisters were upstairs with their door shut. "Get the fuck out of here," he said to me. I clenched my teeth and shook my head. I was between tears and fear. He came closer and stood in front of me. His arm reached out so fast and his hand stopped against my throat. He squeezed hard and pushed me across the room. "Let him go!" my mother screamed as she raced across the room. Now his attention was back on her. His drunken swagger was slowing him down and I started to move quickly into other rooms. I tripped coming around the corner to the front door but managed to get up, look back, and then keep running. "I'll call the cops!" I yelled. I sat out on the front lawn for a while and my mother came outside and said, "He passed out on the couch; come back inside Zechariah." As I entered the house, my mind was scattered with thoughts of my own violence. He was defenseless and I wanted to take advantage. I wanted to inflict pain on him. I didn't want to feel compassion and understand that alcohol was his alter ego. Realizing this made me feel sorry for him. This made me sad, angry, and lonely. If there was anything to suppress the passion in me, it was this. It was this compassionate anger that I held in my heart.

I knew there were hurdles and obstacles to everything I was to do in life. I could accept them, or I could hide from them. I hid from them at times, but soon learned the detriments in doing so. I knew I was passionate when time was removed, when my thoughts were streamlined into good, when my mind was pulsating with energy. I knew that passion was there, I just had to keep at it through desire. Passion was a pure drug in life that I had been addicted to at one time. It faded as I got older, and I hoped to find it again. Passion was an integral piece of my life in order to jump the hurdles.

1995

Family

"Where's your family?" the boy asked. I paused for a while before I spoke. "Not sure, but I know that family is important in life." "How so?" the boy asked. He always had questions about everything. He always made me think. I took the time to think, then answered, "I think family can be anyone we care for, that no matter what happens in life, the end result is that we are safe with them." He looked up at me and smiled. "So my family can also be my friends?" he asked. "Well, ummm, yes, of course, certainly," I responded with another smile. "You see, family to me is a place you can be where love exists both internally and externally," I answered decidedly. He looked at me and smiled again, then rode off on his bike.

He stood so tall and proud

In his suit and tie

His eyes aglow in the candle light

Ryan R. F. Wilkinson

So many Christmases ago

Could it be he was only four?

Such innocence shone

From his little face

Filled with rapture, truth, and grace

Oh, so many years ago

When he was only four

To my Son, one of the ways you have made your imprint on my heart.

Love, Mom, '95

I stood at the top of the stairs, and he was kicking her. Her body lay across three bottom stairs and his leg continued to swing like a hammer trying to break through the wall. Her body was in the way. The noise that came from my mother was reverberating through the stairway and I stood still. I was paralyzed in fear and my brain was trying to process what was going on. During the violence I began to ask myself questions. Why is he doing this? What is he feeling when he acts like this? How will he deal with this situation tomorrow when he realizes what he's done? What demons are within, driving his behaviour? Will he ever stop? Does this being have compassion, remorse, or even a soul underneath his lost self? His eyes were glazed over, the smell of alcohol resonated through the house, and the echoes of pain stirred through my veins. For the first time, I stood and watched until it ended. I froze, watching an event I was all too familiar with. And the next day, I cried until my sadness was only partially removed.

It was our seventh house, and I had made my room reflect who I was with pictures of basketball players, my television set, and video games. The house was older, but had character with all natural wood floors and a different layout. The bathroom had an old fashioned tub, sitting out in the middle of the floor, and in my opinion the sloped ceilings added a touch of coolness. I think I liked this house best out of all the homes we lived in. I felt so lucky to be in this house. The backyard was large and a creek ran across through the back. The creek was peaceful, but I didn't spend enough time there. My mother walked into my room one day and made a strange face, pausing before she spoke. "Zechariah, you've been farting!" she said as she covered her face with her shirt. She shut the door and I laughed so loud it made me continue to fart. I had been lying in bed through the early hours of the morning with the worst stomach ache I could imagine. The next visit to the doctor revealed why I had the aches: I had ulcers. Along with the ulcers came migraines that would debilitate me. Some days I would hold my head tight, pushing it into the pillow. The world around me moved slowly and my eyes focused on nothing. And the smell of my own vomit would remind me that the migraines were real. Stress was building in me.

A week later I was in my room when I heard my mother yell my name. My heart stopped and I could instantly feel my adrenaline kick in. "Zechariah, come outside please," my mother said. "Hold on," I called back. I made my way down the stairs and out the front door. I saw my stepfather unloading a large, long box from the van. "What's that?" I asked. "It's for you, sweetheart," my mother responded. I looked at her perplexed, and I looked at the box. It was an adjustable pole for my basketball backboard and rim. "Really?" I asked. My mother nodded her head and I helped to pull the box out of the van. The gesture filled my heart with warmth. But it was also a mind fuck amidst the peaks and valleys of our family life.

My mother was smart, beautiful, and intelligent. But her life was wearing her down, and I could see how she was changing over the years. She slept more, seemed spaced out more, and worried more. "Zechariah, I think we should leave. I need to take you kids away from your stepfather," she would always say. But there were rarely any actions resulting from these discussions. My mother was an innocent woman, who took complete pride in her children, always watching us from afar with a smile. I often believed that my mother's sole purpose was to garner happiness from her children. I always wondered what she was thinking, how she loved us, and yet sometimes could be a complete stranger. My mother always asked me questions, "Zechariah, why do you listen to those songs, and what do they mean to you?" She asked me to explain myself in great detail so that I myself understood the meaning behind things. She was big on reading and digested books faster than anyone I had ever known. Her generosity and genuine love were pure. At times this confused me, because she would show us how love and family were adorned, and then chaos would happen again. These events, back and forth, shut me down, at times locking my soul away.

My father was strict with me. This turned out to be a good thing. He instilled in me the value of respecting others. I was a smart-ass growing up, but he made sure I was put in my place if I was out of order. He was a great athlete and played hockey for most his life. He worked hard and long hours to provide for his family. He had a bicep that flexed into something bigger than my head. Our relationship was distant in my youth, troubled in my late teens, and reborn in my twenties. My father was smart, handsome, and intelligent. The guy could do a math problem in the blink of an eye. He worked hard, and provided for his family. You could see the kindness through his eyes, pure and full of compassion. Unfortunately, at times his addiction caught up to him. Alcohol seemed to control everyone around me. My mind sorted out a clear distinction between someone who was completely sober and someone who had only had one drink. I knew in their voices over the phone, and I knew in the behaviour they showed in person. I could sense it and I feared it. My father loved to laugh, and he had the goofiest smile that I was lucky enough to be blessed with. Of course, it was only goofy when we were laughing. His heart and love were pure. He was a good man. Outside the alcohol he was a father I strongly admired and trusted.

It was a Saturday afternoon around 12:09 and my friend was on the phone, "Hey, we're going to play basketball at the school with our church group, you in?" "Of course," I responded. One catch: it was hosted by a group who was touring the country promoting religion to youths. Religion was not really my thing, but basketball was. I went. When we arrived there was a group of youth gathered, sitting on the floor. My two friends and I hurried in, and joined them. The man in charge spoke of God and Jesus. "We need to let Jesus into our hearts. Who wants to let Him into your heart?" he asked softly. I looked around and hoped no one would volunteer so we could just get on with playing basketball. Sure enough, he looked at me and asked in front of everyone, "Are you ready to let Jesus into your heart?" My eyes widened and I didn't know how to say no so I nodded and stood up. He let the others shoot around on the gym floor and he took me to the change room. We stood in awkwardness while my friends peeked around the corner. I could see their heads bobbing up and down from the laughter. "Alright, what is your name?" he asked. "Zechariah," I responded slowly. "Repeat after me, Zechariah," he said. I stood and watched his mouth as words came out, and out of the corner of my eye watched my friends continue to laugh. He said some prayer that I didn't understand and I pretended to repeat the words until it was over. This was my first religious experience. I mean, I had gone to church before, but never had something like this happened. And I don't even remember playing basketball that day.

After the 'incident' I started to believe more in my spirituality rather than focusing on religion. But what this threw me into was my family. I thought of the importance of family, not because of the prayer but because of the solitude in a belief system. I started to believe that family could be a foundation. I wanted it to be about my family more than anything else in the world. To this very day I still view family as one of the most important things there are. What a family can give, we can't receive anywhere else. What a family can do is foster growth, courage, a responsibility to protect, provide an ability to fail with acceptance, and most important, the potential to be yourself with your head held high among the clouds. On my end, those things were partially there, but I knew I would have to create them later in life with my own family.

I believed in duty. I believed I had a duty toward certain obligations in my life. I had a duty to put aside the emotional elements, the pain, the selfishness, the complications or repercussions, and deal with the situation in front of me. I believed that I needed to be amiable and fulfill my duty. In my mind, family was a non-negotiable duty. There was no day too busy that I couldn't connect with friends or family in some way. Family was certainly scary, both foreign and familiar.

1996

Health

I lay outside the school yard on the basketball court. I lay on the pavement with my head resting on the ball, looking into the sky. I was content, relaxed, and at peace. A young boy walked past and asked if I wanted to play a game. "No thanks," I said. He then looked up at the sky and asked what I was looking at. "Nothing really, the sky is clear," I responded. The boy looked back down at me and said, "Probably keeps your mind clear also, huh?" I sat up quickly. "Yes, yes it does actually." As he walked away, I noticed he had a hard cough. I stood up, appreciated my health, and kept playing.

In the summer of 1996 I got a job at an old age home. I worked in the Alzheimer's unit and discovered a lot of crazy things that life offered. I discovered that when we get old, it does not get pretty, and I discovered that the more work you put into, well, work, the more you get out of life. Work hard, and the benefits come back to us; work like a lazy, careless person, and nothing comes back. We don't grow or learn if we don't work hard. We don't move forward. Regardless of what I did, it was important to give it my all, because in the end it only came back to me in the form of learning and growth. Attitude was a choice, this I knew, and I was soon learning that if I chose to have a poor attitude in any situation, it would only come back to bite me in the end. So I decided to choose an attitude that was positive in the work I did. I realized also that the health of others suffers as they get older and that is just awful. I was thankful I had my health, thankful I could do the things I chose to do. Let's face it though: I was young, and outside of work I needed to let loose a bit. I needed to let loose a lot. I needed to let loose very much. And so my experience with alcohol and drugs began.

We pulled up to a coffee shop around 8:09 in the evening and sat in the parking lot. Our backs felt as though they were glued to the seats, and all of our hands were stretched out in the middle of the car, pooling our change. We rolled slowly through the drive-thru and I screamed, "We don't have enough; we don't have enough!" So we sped off and regrouped. "Can anyone go in?" I asked. "No way," everyone replied. "Alright, then let's do this again," I responded. We went back to the drive-thru, me in the passenger seat with the money and the three others eagerly awaiting the outcome. "Drive, drive, drive!" I yelled again. My friend hit the gas and we were off. We crept around the corner and came to a stop. We sat and we sat quietly. My eyes locked on the darkness of the sky and I sank deeper and deeper into the seat. My body was part of the car and my mind was numb with the crashing waves of thought. I picked up my hand and felt the strangeness of my skin. It pulsated and talked to me through the veins. My head tingled against the seat and my face morphed into a Picasso painting. I can't be sure how much time passed until finally I came to a conclusion, "Why don't we just get what we can with the money we have?" "Ahhh," said everyone else. "Yes, we will do that." Getting high seemed fun.

A guy at school caught word of our famous adventures with the smoke and asked if he could join us. We planned a night he would certainly remember. We headed to a quarry near town, got out of the car, and began to smoke. My friend took off in the woods nearby, and the rest of us remained at the car. We could hear yelling and running in the woods, which was creating fear in our new companion. When we gathered back into the car, I was in the back seat with the new guy. I looked at him and smiled. "We are taking you somewhere special," I told him. He slouched into the seat and pressed up against the side, trying to create distance from me. We drove for some time and stopped at a gate. The three of us turned to look at the new guy and I said quietly, "We are taking you to your grave." The headlights of the car came back on and we could see the tombstones lined up through the graveyard. His eyes lit up wide and I grabbed his arm. The bumps on the ground rocked the car and the music playing was a fast classical genre, perfect for a graveyard. We stopped halfway in, opened the doors, grabbed him, then dragged him to a tombstone with all the resistance leaving his body. We got to the tombstone, dropped him, and laughed hysterically. He avoided us at school the next day.

As the summer went by, I started to drink. I wanted to know what all the hype was about with alcohol and if I was able to overcome the pull of its demons. It was a test for me. Our parties consisted of straight vodka or rum being consumed in mass quantity. Beer was consumed bottle after bottle until we fell with our bodies limp into the ground. We listened to hard metal and danced until we vomited. Smoking brought out a world I was not meant to be a part of. Many times smoking would lead us to do things that would expand our imaginations or create chaos in our hearts. We played tag in parks, danced, sang, ran, swam, laughed, and let our souls dance on a high wire. Our eyes 'flipped' when we drank. We would look at one another and ask, "Did your eyes flip?" Asking that question meant that we were wondering if the other was at the point of intoxication. Drinking brought out tears, drama and pain for me. Drinking brought out emotions I wasn't yet ready to deal with. I didn't like it so I eventually stopped. And while I enjoyed the fun, I knew that it was not for me. Interestingly enough, I could recount in detail the times I spent drunk or high, but I can't remember too much about my sober days. What a shame. And that is what some would call the great times in their lives, when in reality they were holding themselves back.

There came a time when I needed to realize that sobriety was important. It was necessary to be clear minded, especially when horrific events happened in my life. If I continued to hide reality through drugs and alcohol, my state of mind would grow pain rather than killing it off. Alcohol and drugs can stall our state of mind. They circulate unwanted thoughts and nullify logic. I knew altering my mind was fun in the moment, but I also knew it was only for a short time. I knew I didn't want to be like my parents when it came to what I put in my body. I wanted health in my life, both mental and physical. Although alcohol brought people together, it destroyed them individually.

When I focused on my health, I was better equipped to challenge life through clear thinking, strong instinct, and a foundation of pure thought. There was a freedom that came with health. When I focused on my health it provided the tools to carry my body through life with an endurance I couldn't otherwise have had. Health is what led me to a smile, helping me realize that I had the strength to always overcome. Health was vital if I was to overcome. It was all in my hands. Health was entirely my choice.

1997

Sacrifice

I arrived home to find nothing. Everything was gone. There was a child walking in the summer heat. He looked at me and asked why I was in such a panic. I had no response. He had with him some hockey cards and asked if I collected any. "I used to, but they are all gone now," I responded. He said, "Sometimes we trade, and sometimes we get nothing in return." Sacrifice was a bitter pill to swallow, especially when I didn't know what I was trading.

I stood with my friends outside my house, in a circle on the street. We rarely made eye contact and we certainly didn't say much. We stood for what felt like a day. No cars came by to break us up and there was no place to be other than here. We knew it was the last hurrah from our days in that town, and we knew it was a goodbye. We may have feared the possibility that it was goodbye forever. But it wasn't. My friends and I stood outside my house, on the street, moving on to college, university, work, and whatever life had prepared for us. Twenty minutes passed as we stood silently, then we shook hands, we hugged, and we wished each other the best. The silence from that circle of friends that night has rang through my mind ever since. The silence was the loudest part. It enclosed us in an ongoing relationship and was solidified through our bond. We knew the bond was strong, and we understood we had something special that would last forever. We also knew that each of us was willing to sacrifice for the sake of our friendship.

In 1997 my mother achieved what I thought was the impossible. She left my stepfather. For the first time, we had a home, as a peaceful family, without fear or worry about what was going to happen. 6:09, the morning of our first day in the new house, my mother screamed, "Zechariah! Zechariah!" I awoke and immediately ran downstairs, skipping all but three of the twelve stairs. There he was, dressed in a long green army coat, as the smell of booze entered the house. I latched onto his coat with both hands at his chest and started fighting. I didn't have time to listen to my heart racing nor did I have time to understand what was happening. Instinct took over and there I was, in a battle in the kitchen of our first house away from him. My sister stood in the living room watching everything. "Let's see what you got, kid," he said. I actually smiled because I knew I had been waiting a long time for this. "I got lots, you fucking idiot!" I yelled. My peripheral caught my younger sister's image standing and watching the whole event. All I could do was toss him around the kitchen and into the fridge, the stove, and the freezer. Back and forth through the kitchen we went. My hands clasped on his jacket; his hands were on my skin. I don't remember how it stopped. My mother was in the kitchen the entire time and managed to avoid us. He reached out to shake my hand and I closed the door. "Fuck all of you!" he yelled as he walked past the front of the house. I walked over to the door and stepped out onto the street. He began to walk faster down the road, and there I was in my boxers, asking him to come back. I felt enlightened. I could finally defend my family and myself, and I wanted more. He vanished down the street, and I went inside, hugged my mother and sister, and told them it was over. I was in control.

A few months after that incident my mother, due to the cycles she only knew, met another man who was similar to my stepfather. It was a Monday afternoon and my mother was nowhere to be found. She was missing for days. I contacted a friend of hers who told me that my mother was at a motel with her new boyfriend. I needed to eat; I needed money. I needed my mother back. I found myself home alone most days, with my younger sister at her father's and my older sister out of town, and I was wondering what to do. I had rage inside me building and I snapped. I was lost in the thought of the cycle continuing. I had anger to fight a hundred men. I was lost and I was scared. I was young. I drove up to the motel and sat in my car, staring at the door. I got out and went up to the room, but before I could knock, a man came out in a white tank top. I walked past him and there were two others. "Where is she?!" I screamed. My mother came out of the washroom, "Zechariah, what are you doing here?" "What do you mean? What do you mean what am I doing here? Where have you been? What the fuck is going on?" I turned around and could see a man coming at me. He went to grab me and I pushed him down. I drove my elbow into his chest as he squirmed, trying to get out of my grip. I drove my fist into his face and finally got up off the floor. I walked out of the room and he got up to follow me. Outside he stood at the doorway. "Who the fuck are you to come into my house?" he yelled. "Nice house, asshole," I responded. I told him if he came near me I would be driving him to the hospital after the fact. I got in my car, and drove off. When I got home I knew it was all over. I reflected on what just happened, and

I began to feel like I was slowly demonstrating similar behaviours of the people I fought with. I had to change that. I had to leave.

Shortly after that incident I got a job on the railway, swinging sledge and doing odd tasks along the track. The job was situated far north and we would get up around five in the morning and come back to the motel around eight every night. On weekends we'd go home for two days, then back to work on Monday. There were probably ten of us at any given time and the thought of working with those guys again makes me cringe. "Hey, you fuck heads, get back and fix those anchors on the plates," my boss would yell. "I will replace every last fucking one of you," he'd add in a serious undertone. I looked at him and wondered how the hell he got away with talking to us like that. We walked back over to the cart that carried our material and noticed it was moving slowly on its own. "Hey, the cart's getting away!" one of the guys yelled. "Holy shit, stop it before it takes off!" another guy yelled. I looked to my left and one of the workers picked up a sixty-pound pry bar and ran after the cart. He ran beside the cart and then daggered the pry bar into the spokes of the wheel, as he held on. I saw his feet in the air as he flipped over and landed on his back. The other guys were laughing and I just stood there staring at him. The cart got away and was found up the track. I knew we were in deep shit. The only good things out there were the scenery, fresh air, and appreciation for hard work. I mean, this was gruesome, and the turnover of workers seemed hourly. On my last day, our boss made us replace track we had already done and I went back to the truck to get my lunch before we started. "What makes you so fucking special?" he said. "Absolutely nothing," I replied. I grabbed my hard hat and drop kicked it into the air. "But you can take that back," I added. I stood there with no hard hat, and then realized I needed a ride home.

One time my key didn't work when I arrived home. I went around to the side door but the key didn't work there either. I went to a friend's house to use the phone and called my mother. No answer. I finally reached her at her friend's house. "Zechariah, we lost the house. The landlord took everything." "Mom, that was our home, it was our home, Mom," I said, broken hearted. All my possessions were gone. Everything I owned was gone. Toys, pictures, clothing, and anything I had collected over the years were gone. The landlord had locked up the house and gotten rid of everything. I thought hard about what had transpired. Then I thought about all the belongings and what they meant to me. As much as my tears fell, I had to dig deep in my soul to understand that these items could be replaced. I thought about the life in front of me and decided that at least no one could take that from me. No one could decide anymore what I would do with my future. I was homeless, but I knew I would survive. I lived in my car for two weeks, frequently making trips to the trunk where I kept peanut butter and bread. I needed a place where I could focus on my remaining years as a teenager. I needed a place where I could have teenage worry and teenage drama, and not the drama of lost adults. My friend's mother offered to take me in, and without hesitation, I accepted. It was one of the best decisions I made as a teenager. Without her help, I wouldn't have gone on the path I did.

I was in survival mode. School didn't occur to me, relationships didn't occur to me, and life was not clicking for me. I didn't know what was happening. I didn't understand, and I searched for answers but found none. Life is such a fast blur in the teenage years, it's hard to remember everything, especially when I didn't want to. However, I would understand for the rest of my life that possessions, unlike people, can come and go easily. Sometimes when we surround ourselves with plastic, cement, steel, and material things, we drift from humanity and live life from the outside in, rather than from the inside out.

Christmas morning of 1997 I was awakened by my aunt. She told me my mother was in the hospital and that my uncle was coming to take me there. I didn't think anything of it because my mother was in and out of hospitals often at this point. My uncle came quite quickly, and my aunt and grandmother were in the car. "Merry Christmas, how are you?" I asked everyone. They just kind of moved their heads a bit in response. We arrived at the hospital and the doctor came over to us with the news. The doctor finished speaking, and then it hit me. "What?" I asked rhetorically. My uncle leaned in and said sternly, "Your mother is comatose, Zechariah." "No one told me that!" I screamed back. By the end of the day, my cousin and some of my close friends had arrived. I entered my mother's room quietly, as though I could wake her if I was noisy. I looked at the nurse and asked, "Could you please give me some time in here?" She left. I looked down at my mother and I looked at her arms, noticing they were covered in scars. My hand on hers, I leaned in, "Mom, maybe you can hear me, maybe you can't. Either way, I want you to know that I love you very much. Please don't leave me now. Don't go. Don't do this now. We have so much to do, so much to make up for and so much to build." I didn't yet know why she was there or what happened. My mind wandered toward a self inflicted suicide attempt, and unfortunately I was right. Later she would tell me why: "I was looking at the Christmas tree and all the lights, then looked down at my coffee mug and decided I didn't deserve it." "Didn't deserve what?" I asked. "The mug," she said. "I threw it through the window and then took the rest of my prescription drugs. I watched the lights on the tree until I fell asleep." I knew my mother's mental health was declining, but I hadn't known to what extreme. Or maybe I just wanted to ignore it.

After that incident my mother was in and out of a psychiatric hospital. In the same year, my father checked into a detox clinic. I didn't quite understand what was happening around me, but I tried. My mother wrote me letters often, attempting to break through my young mind. Did it work at the time? No, but later on, the words would resonate through me.

My Darling Sweet Zechariah,

How hard your life has been. My soul aches for answers and I pray for a better life for you. I want to thank you for being you, so wonderful, loving, generous, and understanding. I'm sorry that I could not give you a better life but I couldn't love you more, that is forever and endless. Actually I love you more each day of my life. That's all I can give you. I hope it's enough for now. My love, my support, my respect for you is immense. My darling Zechariah, you are a blessing sent to me. Remember though, that I still am the parent although the roles sometimes get reversed. I will always take care of you to the best of my ability. As you know, we can only do what we can when we are ready. I'm sorry I wasn't ready sooner; however, time has its own reason. Be strong and yet don't hide your feelings. Be who you are, who you want to be. Don't let anyone take that away or try to, as you may end up messed up like myself. It's going to be a rough road, life is not easy and the choices you make, please make them very carefully. I love you Zechariah and miss you. I hope to be home soon. I'll work as best that I can, as hard as I can until my emotions say to rest. I've made some bad choices in my life, but also some good ones. It's the good ones I try to focus on. My children are everything to me and I hate to let you down or disappoint you, although I know I love you and I am sorry. However, I am a living, breathing, feeling person as well.

Zechariah, please seek therapy. Don't wait, because then there's more to deal with and it's easier to make wrong choices.

I trust you and love you very much.

Mom

xxxx
oooo

I understood my mother was not just a mother but a person also. I knew I needed to forgive her and let go of my anger if I was to move on in my life. One fact remained; she was caught between heaven and hell.

In time I also understood that I needed to see a therapist. It was on a Friday afternoon when I found myself sitting in a waiting room that was full of blank walls. "Zechariah, nice to meet you," the therapist said as he reached out to shake my hand. "Come on in." I walked into the room and asked if I could sit down. "Of course, take a seat," he replied. His eyes were full of light and we sat and looked each other up and down briefly. He asked, "So, Zechariah, what do you want to get out of these sessions?" I took a while to respond, because I didn't know. I could feel myself fabricating a false reality. I wanted to cry, shout, rage, and punch a hole through the wall. My thoughts raced through my veins, creating a time bomb of emotion. "I am looking to get out of my situation," I responded calmly. "What situation are you in, Zechariah?" "My family is violent and fucking crazy. There is alcohol, drugs, and violence, and I can't deal with it. I don't know how. I am lost. I need help." There was silence for a long time after I spoke. "Can I swear in here?" I asked. "Yes, you can swear if you like," he answered. "Alright, but seriously, what do I do about this?" He grabbed a pamphlet and handed it to me. I took a deep breath. "Sorry, I'm gonna go," I said without eye contact. At times I felt like I was living a lie based on how people downplayed the events that surrounded me. I felt as though I shouldn't be sad or angry and I felt guilt for it. Why did I feel guilt? Why did I feel as though all these events were being diluted by others? This was a real situation and my voice needed to be heard.

If I had the choice, would I have taken this adventure in life? Would I have listened carefully to the words of the wise, the elderly, and those who also understood sacrifice? If I was given a list of all the troubles, tribulations, successes, deaths, births, ups, downs, and sacrifices of what life is, would I have chosen to endure it? Would I have jumped in? It was sacrifice that led me to balance the direction of my hope. I never gave up. I knew I needed to talk to someone. I needed to have a real interaction about the events that had unfolded in front of me. I knew that I needed to give up something in order to overcome. I believed and realized that I needed to continue suffering in order to find clarity. I figured that life is a sacrifice. I knew that sacrifice in my life would lead me to appreciate. I was good with that sacrifice.

1998

Wisdom

In 1998, I found myself in art school. I drew, painted, drafted, sculpted, and creatively danced through the courses. Art was becoming something very personal to me. I knew I didn't want to do it as a career, but just for my own growth. I was in the hallway of the school sitting by a window drawing when a young student approached me. "What are you drawing?" he asked. "The sun," I answered. "I love when the sun rises every day. It's a fresh start," he told me. I mentioned that was very wise of him to say, and he completed the sentence for me. "It was wisdom that opened the doors to appreciate the sun in the first place."

Although I think experience is great, each individual's experience is unique. Wisdom is no different. It's how you apply wisdom through experience in your life that leads to success. I felt change was happening all around me, although I had yet to find my perfect direction. At times, anger was still fuelling my life. I lived and breathed it. I knew that it needed to change and had to be controlled if I wanted to move forward. I decided to live with my father and commute to art school in 1998. I was there alone most times, because he travelled back and forth to his girlfriend's house outside of the city.

One day while commuting to school at 10:09 in the morning, driving fast and carelessly down the road, I found myself stopped at the scene of a car accident. There were two cars, a red car on the road facing me, and a grey car partially in the ditch about forty feet away. As I drove closer, I realized it was bad. I parked on the side of the road, called the police, and then got out of my car. I noticed someone in the grey car moving, talking, and aware of what was happening. I quickly walked over and told the woman help was on the way. "Please don't move!" I said. She nodded, and then I made my way over to the red car. The front end was crunched up so much that the front seats of the car touched the dashboard, the steering wheel was planted into the chest of the man inside, and pieces of the car were scattered all over the road. As I walked closer to the car, I noticed the man inside had his head turned toward the window, looking out. I finally approached the car, and I noticed that half his head was through the windshield. I slowed my walk and went up to the driver-side window. He was staring at me, with his eyes open, lifeless. I took some time to look at him, and soon realized he was dead. His eyes remained in the moment, only seconds before; pondering his life, carrying on with his day. I felt like I could see his soul, understanding the peace that came with his death. It was silent, serene, and sad at the same time. Who would suffer because of his death? What family did he have? What was his story? Who was he? I looked at him again, "I'm so sorry," I whispered. This event instilled the wisdom in me that death could arrive at any moment. For the first time, I accepted death, and for the first time I accepted the reality that we are not here for eternity. I was not invincible; it was merely a matter of time before I would die. Why am I so engaged in the past when my future could be stopped tomorrow? What memories did I want flashing before me when death arrived?

That summer I realized I needed something to replace my ongoing thoughts of the past, to keep me moving forward mentally and physically. I knew I needed a better challenge. I needed something that could bring me to another level in my life by pushing me forward. I needed something to take me out of my comfort zone. I began lifting weights at the gym where I unleashed hell. What the gym did for me was give me strength, energy, confidence, and a newfound control that was structured in a way I had never experienced. It was just me against the weights in my hands. If I didn't eat right, it pushed back harder than I wanted. If I didn't sleep right, then the weights won the battle of resistance. The pain searing through my muscles could eventually stop me from continuing. It could prevent me from doing battle against the iron again and again. It could also immobilize me the next day from the wear and tear, but in a good way. When I was pushing and pulling the iron, it was if I was pushing and pulling my life with pure control. I grew stronger and more resilient through every repetition. I was building a fortress where pain was all but accepted. If I placed structure and consistency in my life I would not only overcome the iron, but also life. The iron taught me lessons I wouldn't have otherwise learned about my ability to keep pushing, no matter what the circumstance.

I'm not sure why I eventually chose working out in a gym over basketball. Basketball had brought me such escape. Was it time to move on? Was it time to take the next step? Did I realize that change was the only thing keeping me alive in this world? Possibly, yes, and possibly I knew that I needed change. In life, I realized it was important to follow my heart and passions. I was to

103

find a way to be in tune with my gut, and follow its lead regardless of my own personal fear and resistance. It was like these changes in direction kept me alive. The gym was exactly what I needed to clear my mind, body, and soul. I was healthy and I wanted to keep it that way. I knew that the healthier my body was, the healthier my mind was going to be. I also knew I was starting to build my armour, my safety net from the world. What I also realized was that strength was great, but wisdom and knowledge were better. People know how to deal with violence through violence. But when we use our minds, the violence fades and life can become something real and meaningful. My mind, not violence, needed to carry me onward.

As I got older, anxiety found a way to disrupt my life repeatedly. It had been learned at an early age and was only getting worse. Anxiety was a familiar place when I was a kid, built on the foundation of fear. Wisdom was something I figured could lead to more options and choices. Those choices were enabling me to deal with my anxiety. Wisdom led me to understand my fears. Fear could stop me in life. It could alter who I was, define me, and manipulate my mind. Sometimes I needed to void the past in order to do the right thing in the present. If I held onto the past and all its demons, it could blur my vision in the present. I knew that wisdom would carry me through. I had to be smarter than the events in front of me. I had learned that my momentum in life would steer me in the right direction if I was smart about it. I had to constantly evolve, and I had to constantly learn new ways to overcome the anxiety.

One afternoon I was sitting on the couch, looking at the sky through the balcony glass doors. Suddenly screams filled the air and articles of clothing raced passed my line of sight. I got up and walked over to the balcony to see what was going on. I looked seven stories down and there he was. "Fuck you, bitch!" he was screaming as his stuff was thrown out of the building. I looked up and saw her arms hanging over the balcony and I asked, "Do you need help?" She laughed and two minutes later she knocked on my door. "Hey, come on in," I said as I opened the door. "Are you okay?" I asked. Though we had never met previously, she walked in and sat down. "I'm sorry you had to see that," she said. "No problem," I responded. "I don't know what the hell I'm doing anymore. I don't know what to do or who to trust. Mind if I smoke?" she said as she lit a cigarette. I sat down beside her. "Direction in life is really determined by self-control and insight. It's garnered through a wisdom learned from events like today," I said. She looked at me, stunned. "The more we can see the picture outside of the frame, the more we can put into perspective, and the more we can put into perspective, the more we are able to deal with. And sometimes we don't truly see the opportunity in front of us amidst the chaos," I said. "That sounds fucked," she said back to me. "But I see your point. What you are saying, I guess it holds wisdom," she finally said before standing up. "Maybe it does, maybe it doesn't; what do I know?" I said. "I just hope that fucker rots in hell," she said. I laughed and walked her out. "I am here if you need anything at all," I told her. She thanked me and then shut the door.

When school ended I needed to leave my father's apartment and get back to my friends. I knew that there are places that can be poisonous and places that can nurture and push you forward. Unfortunately that was not where I was. But in time maybe I could return to that place with a different approach or feeling. What was evident to me was that I needed to be where my friends were. I didn't think twice about it. I picked up and moved and arrived at the place I should have been all along. My smile came back that very day. It was a wise move.

Time was moving faster as I aged. Were the events in my life aging me faster? I had always felt that time was my enemy, but now I decided that time was merely the passing of thought pushing experience through memory. I felt that time was able to collect wisdom for me, so I figured it was a good thing. This was exciting.

I had the wisdom to understand that it was not my fault that unfortunate things happened through my youth, but rather a series of events out of my control which shook my world harder than I could have imagined. To continue shaking would mean that the grasp of these events were holding me back. I soon realized that part of my success in my life was because I drew healthy wisdom from good and bad experiences. I was also in a place where it was now up to me to be in control. I searched for eternity, unknowingly stumbled, and found that time carried wisdom back to what found me.

1999

Love

Death is funny. To me it really was. Out of nervousness I laughed when people died, though I normally cried when no one was looking. I cried when I watched commercials and I cried when someone else was in pain. A young boy came up to me in the hospital and asked, "Is your wife having a baby?" "No," I replied while chuckling to myself, "my grandfather is very sick." "Is he going to be fine?" the boy asked. "Not sure," I replied. "We can only hope," the young boy said. He started to walk down the hall and then stopped briefly to say one last thing before he left: "Whatever happens, people will be fine if you love them."

I stood silently for a moment, looking at everyone sitting in the church. It was 3:09 in the afternoon. I scanned the room and saw familiar faces. It was warm and the silence was comforting. I looked at his casket then looked at the paper in front of me. I took a deep breath, exhaled, and then I read my eulogy:

I stand here today to pour my heart out to a man who has made me very proud to call my grandfather. I would like to share my memory of him. His sincerity brought smiles and warmth. His arms were open and inviting at all times. His patience showed he cared. His gentle ways and kind heart made me feel loved and cherished. He is the only man I knew who never stopped smiling. He judged no one and accepted everyone. For a long time I looked at the world in black and white. He taught me how to see the world in colour. It is as though he lived his life to strengthen ours. His art...can show us beauty of life through his eyes. There is a part of his soul in every painting. The brilliant colours he used amaze me every time I see them. He was not only my grandfather, but a friend and a hero. Knowing him was one of the most precious things in my life. There are very few people that impact lives the way he did, and yet he kept a sense of humour until the day he left us. If only the rest of the world had this love and passion for life. I am honoured to have had such a beautiful person in my life. I will continue to learn from him for the rest of my life. I will never forget the man I want to be and he will live in my heart forever. I will miss you dearly, my friend.

After my speech, I cried; I cried hard. It was during this two-week span of hospital visits and mourning that I understood love. Love to me was something evolving. Although as a child I was not shown pure love all the time, I began to finally understand what it was. I thought for some time, and decided I wanted to give the love that my soul devoured, and let my heart dance for a change. I felt that I had ignored the beauty around me, and that was a mistake. I needed to observe, absorb, and replenish love lost from my life. I needed to ensure I carried love through to my own future family. I needed to carry it with me for the remainder of my life, and the only way I could do that was to accept it. I believed I needed to carry out my grandfather's beauty. To be surrounded by his ideas and his ways was important. At the funeral they had set up some of his paintings and wood carvings. There it was, on a stand, one of my grandfather's rare wood carvings. It was a face - old, wrinkled, and almost Native Indian - that looked at me while I gave my grandfather's eulogy. It was a lost spirit in search of meaning, and was clearly the face from the window years before. I paused briefly, startled. I came to love and respect that face, regardless of its meaning that I knew nothing of. It provided me with a comfort that I can't explain. Sometimes I would never know the meaning of things. I would just have to accept this.

A week after the funeral, I sat at home with a friend. We had a few beers and he asked me how I felt about my grandfather's death. "How did it feel when he passed, Zechariah?" he asked. "Well, death seemed to just creep up without warning. It was weird to see him in the hospital like that in a clear mental state, but with his body shutting down on him, in atrophy," I responded. "Yeah, that's messed up," my friend said. I continued, "The physical pain I felt while he was dying was immense. I was just aching all over every single night. And I can't help but think he is watching over me, as cliché as that sounds." "Did you talk to him when he was dying?" my friend asked. I was buzzing from the beer and didn't hold back. "Yeah, I sure did. I said 'Pappa, we all love you so much.' He grabbed my hand tightly and said, 'I know Zechariah, I know.' He heard the music we played for him. He saw the art we placed around the hospital room, and he was kept warm under the wool blanket from home. He passed on to the next life knowing the love would never end. His death helped me discover love." My friend sat and stared at me, so I changed the direction of the conversation, "Let me grab you another beer then let's head out to see some ladies." He agreed.

To me, love was unexplainable. Did I understand it? Not really. Would I be able to explain it one day? Maybe. But I knew in my heart that I had so much love to give and there were many ways to do it. My grandfather expressed his love in many ways, including his art. To me that was on par with how I would like to express myself. Art was a way to showcase love from within. Art was true love because it came from passion. And it was the part of him that others could see.

I knew I wanted to experience love. I wanted to love someone with all my passion, heart, and soul. I wanted to figure it out, and experience it. I wondered if I had become so starved of love in my life that I was blind when it was in front of me. I wanted to let my walls down. Relationships with women were hard in my life. I would build a wall that was at most times impenetrable. I would always find a way out. Most times I would view romantic relationships as someone secretly trying to figure me out so they could cut me down and hurt me, find all my weaknesses and use them against me. I thought all they wanted to do was put me in my place and reassure me that I was nothing much. I thought they were possibly going to do what my parents did to me: let me suffer. Externally I was bullet proof. Internally I would crumble without anyone knowing. The mask would stay on and I would make myself believe what I said. Sometimes I would tell myself that I was fine when I wasn't. Sometimes I would tell myself I was healthy when I wasn't. Sometimes I would tell myself that people love me, when maybe I doubted that all along. There was always truth to my words; however, there was doubt in my truth because I never felt I had the support to follow through. I never looked in someone else's eyes and felt that I believed. I never felt that love was real. From an early age, love was a gamble in my world. I needed to understand love by allowing myself to be loved. I knew that love was the most important thing to have. I knew that love was going to be a struggle to accept, but the reward of trusting in love was greater than I knew or could understand.

I also knew that it would take time for me to accept love, and in turn, give love. Sometimes I didn't know where I was or where I was going, and that's when I needed to listen to my heart.

2000

Soul

I stumbled up to the gate of my house, tripping over the stone set in the grass. I regained my balance, and looked up. There was that boy who was always so interested in life. "Where've you been?" he asked. "I've been around," I replied. "Well, I haven't seen you in months, and your eyes, they seem empty." "My eyes are empty?" I asked. "It looks like you are missing something in your life," said the boy. I sat down, and answered as best I could. "Sometimes we get lost in our lives and the space grows. Sometimes we live in a world that we really aren't part of." The young boy asked his final question of the day: "So does that mean we aren't real?" I smiled and told the boy, "We are very real. At times we look at the world from the outside in because we may feel we don't belong. We can lose connection with our soul."

It was 8:09 in the evening when the phone rang. My mother was on the other end, "Zechariah, he has a gun. Please help me." I froze for a brief second then responded, "You have to get out of there. What do you mean he has a gun?" She answered more quietly, "He has a shotgun under the boards in the floor and said he was going to use it on me." "Alright, call the cops, Mom, call the cops, alright?" I spoke quickly. Her silence was growing. "Mom…Mom……MOM!" The phone was dead. I sat on the bed and clenched my fist, then unleashed it through the wall. I called the police. Eventually my mother got in touch and told me what happened, and that her boyfriend would be spending time in prison. "This is it," she explained, "Now is the time for me to leave." I responded to her claim she would leave and told her I would be there in a second. "Let's do this, Mom, let's get this done." But she would never leave. This was her past repeating over and over and over again. She was too sick to understand and too lost to follow through. I don't doubt my mother loved him, and that is why she stayed. This was her weakness. She cared too much about people who chose to do harm in return.

Shortly after the shotgun incident I got another phone call. This time my mother called from a pay phone, "Zechariah, I need your help, please." Her voice weakened and I could hear the tears streaming down her face. "My veins collapsed and I have no money to do anything," she said through her tears. "What? You are shooting drugs? Mom, you need to go to the hospital immediately; what the hell are you doing?" I responded. She was broken, destroyed, and the only thing holding us together was the phone line. "I love you so much, Mom, but you need to go to the hospital. I can't do anything else for you right now." "Save yourself; this troubled mind may be gone tomorrow," she finally said. And then I heard a click. I never knew if my mother made it to the hospital. Our next conversation was like nothing had ever happened, and she pretended that life was great. Often after our phone conversations I would cry. It was painful and it took all my strength to gather my thoughts.

I understood my life was becoming a paradox, but only to a certain extent. I understood how I would vanish mentally, and it would seem as though I wasn't even there. I knew I was real, and the events were real; however, I didn't understand why I sometimes vanished. The paradox of life was wrapped around me. I would be present without really being in the moment. My sadness crept out, and my laughter was hidden. There were no mentors, nor parents that really understood what I needed, nor did I understand the direction I was going. I began to wonder who I really was. I wondered, doubted, and second guessed my very existence. I craved to be loved. While growing up, love was pushed so far deep down that it felt like my soul had been removed. I was struggling yet again with understanding love. I wanted to trust that love was real. I wanted to feel it. I wanted it so badly, but at this point, I didn't know how to accept it and I didn't understand what love to trust. When someone looked me in the eyes and told me they loved me, I didn't want to have to struggle to believe them. I wanted to trust what they said. I wanted my soul to accept it. I wanted to believe in it. I wanted to learn how to believe in it, but it scared me.

My soul was eaten away, and I had lost my capacity to understand what was normal. I had to relearn simple social skills. I had to learn how to be affectionate in relationships. I had to learn how to make decisions that were so simple for other people. Simple things in life that everyone else could do without thinking were a struggle for me. My gas tank was low; all the fuel had been used up in my youth. Where do I go? What do I become? I was anxious while talking to people, walking out into a crowd, and even speaking to people in conversation. I had internal doubts about everything. I would go to sleep thinking about a simple word someone used in a conversation with me, and try to analyze it because I thought it held another meaning that was negative.

To let my life flow freely through time, I had to learn how to understand the dynamics of people, and adapt accordingly. I had to find my soul again; I had to dig deep down within and find spirituality. I had to. I had to in order to survive. Without notice, I would break down emotionally and let it all go, these years of suppressed anger and sadness spilling over into reality. Through all of these awkward events, they highlighted what I needed to focus on in my life. They highlighted areas to improve upon and I know I needed to develop them in order to function with some normalcy.

Now I had to make a conscious effort to re-involve myself into the life that surrounded me. I had always felt that I should send the message that I had all the time in the world for anyone. If a child came to a father, the child should sense that his father has all the time in the world available for him. I also felt that you should never carry your stresses with you, because then they are passed onto those you interact with. My mind whispered to me each night before I went to bed, whispering the struggles and the tiredness. It called my name and it told me to shut off.

Fortunately for me, with my friends, the paradox seemed to fade. They accepted me for who I was in the moment, and that allowed me to enter life, knowing that I was real to them, and in turn, real to myself. The paradox was strong, but my friends were stronger and I felt I belonged. I felt as if my soul understood what my mind didn't at the time. Older than my body, my soul would not let me down.

Great souls endure in peaceful environments. You need to forgive yourself, forgive others, and move forward to bring the reality of peace. I needed to drive my compassion toward others, to continue being me, and to continue being there for the people

I cared about. I needed to continue to push my ego aside in order to do so.

My father was on the phone and we were arguing. "Zechariah, you chose to go to school and you have to pay that debt," he said. "But I am trying, I just need help Dad, I need help to get on my feet," I responded. I was nervous enough asking my father for help, because it was something I had never done, and I never wanted to. "Well, I think you should find a job and get back on your feet then. It's your life and you should go live it," he said, insinuating that there was going to be a greater distance between us at this point. I put the phone down and went to my room. I stared out the window and a few tears rolled down my face.

I woke up the next day with thoughts of my father and our conversation still in my mind. I left the house early without breakfast, and I made my way down to the water on the edge of town. It was a Saturday, and there were lots of people making their way around and through the area where I was sitting. I watched each person closely. I wondered where each soul was going, who they were, what their stories were, and what kind of people they were. I observed a small child with his father only a few feet away, smiling, playing, and entirely in peace. I wondered what their story was. I began to observe their dynamics, their behaviours, and their interactions. I wondered what the father thought of his son, and I wondered what the son thought of his father. As I watched more people around me, I began to think of my own father, my life, and the decisions I had control over. I figured out that my soul should still be connected to the only father I had. I took a break from people watching, and I decided to write my father a letter:

Dad,

You are who you are, and I am who I am. This we can both agree on. I know I have not been perfect in my life, nor have I been the ideal son that I know I could be. There is a lot of pain, hurt, and sadness within me and I want to fix it. I want to change it and become better in my life. The things that are important to me may not be important to you, but I want you by my side as a father should be. I want to be by your side as a son should be. My life has many years left and what a waste if you weren't in it. The love between a father and son should be endless. We should be a team that ensues through the challenges, standing shoulder to shoulder no matter what. I love you with everything I have. I hope one day you will understand what I am about and see me for what my intentions are in this life. I want nothing but positive things for you always and I can't wait to see what the world unfolds for us in the future. At the end of the day, all I ever want is for you to be proud of me.

Love, Zechariah

There were days when I knew I was connected to my soul. And there were days I knew I wasn't. My soul to me is a connection with my inner spirit and inner voice, recognizing that there are sometimes two of us in one person. My soul has carried me through life with love and my soul knows no boundaries. My soul can help me be free. I couldn't be free with what was left inside of me. I needed to free my soul from the past. I knew my soul was seeking something different in the world. My soul was singing to me through my thoughts and actions. I just needed to pay attention. I needed to understand.

I knew I needed to connect to my soul if I was to follow the path it led me to. My soul was my guide.

2001

Learn

I was in the library and my mind was wandering. I was lost, distracted, and bored all at the same time. I looked out the window at the snow slowly falling and thought it was peaceful. My mind was distant and my body damaged from a hard gym workout the day before. There was a young man sitting across from me. "Tired?" he asked. "I am very tired," I responded. "Have you ever taken a real break, like, a break from life?" he asked. "What are you talking about?" He smiled and responded, "It's important to take a break from hardships in life. It's important to let your mind rest, and recuperate. We need to stop, and reflect on every hardship, and reflect on what we've learned in order to move forward." I didn't disagree. I nodded and went on about my day. Later, it occurred to me: I needed to rest. But what did I need a rest from? The answer was simple…I needed a rest from the world I knew. If I was to continue to learn, I had to be a student elsewhere.

In 2001 I found myself attending college again. 2:09 on a November afternoon and I was sitting in a classroom, but I was really somewhere else. This feeling of displacement was a common theme at this point in my life. At the end of class, the professor came up and asked if she could talk to me alone. The others left the room and I sat perched on a desk. "You seem very sad, Zechariah." "Why do you say that?" I wondered. She replied to me with words that seemed to wrap around the truth. "Your eyes tell me you're sad, scared, distant maybe?" I knew it was the truth, but I wasn't ready to hear it. I told her I was going through some things, and would be fine. "It seems to me that the sadness is layered of many years," she quietly said back to me. She was right. The thing was, I couldn't learn anymore. My mind was too full from the memories of the years before. It was stalled in the past. I knew nothing of world events. I knew nothing of any relevance anymore. I didn't have the capacity to even digest information from my text books. I realized my mind had been consumed by my past, my chaotic thoughts, and memories. My fuel tank was empty, and I couldn't make a decision about my life. I knew I needed to keep learning, and growing, but how?

I was twenty-three and my mind checked out of school. I know now it was probably because I wasn't passionate about what I was doing. I decided to take some downtime to reflectively think about my life and where I was heading. I needed to do investigating in other areas. I needed to think about who I was, who I had become, and why I was who I was. I needed to look at myself as I was at that moment, and in present time. I started dreaming again of good things, like art, people, and ideas. This transition was good for me. One powerful thought crossed my mind and that was forgiveness. I had played with this idea before, but now I began to realize it was essential. I thought that if I could forgive everyone in my life who had caused me pain, maybe the weight would lift off and I could find my way again. Maybe that was the key to being able to learn again. Maybe I needed to change myself, my way of thinking, my approach. If I learned to forgive, the pain might surface, and then I would be able to deal with it and move on. I realized I needed to allow the pain to surface, in order to deal with it, and then in turn be free to move on with my life. Swallow the bitterness, as the monks once said. Sometimes society dictates one life and we live another behind closed doors. So why hide behind the confinement of society in order to make changes? My past had been violent, but my future lay silent until I found a way to make it sing. Why hide what I had been through? Why not lay it out in front of me, and deal with it the best I can?

My friend called me that evening with good news. He had been very successful in his academic endeavours and was being rewarded with a full scholarship. It didn't surprise me at all, but rather made me significantly happier knowing that my friend's success brought me joy. He succeeded in himself and he also succeeded in me. The exchange was good. Our conversation continued for quite some time. He asked, "How are things with the family?" And I replied, "Well, they are what they are I guess." He continued to pry a bit more and asked if I ever regretted anything from those past years. I told him that I would only regret something if I made the same mistake twice. To me, regret would come from the repetition of my mistakes, which could place me in a cycle of regret, or force me to wish I had done something different with my life. I knew I built many walls, but if I chose to have no walls, maybe I could have a full view of the world and learn something. My friend's reaction was a long pause. "Well then I am happy for you!" he shouted into the phone. I laughed a bit and told him to piss off.

As the year went by, my mind continued to open up. I thought deeply and I realized many things. I could understand something only so far, and then there would be change. Everything in life can change, adapt, contort, and grow, and then I needed to learn it again. That's why I needed to constantly grow, develop, learn, and become amiable. I needed to be open to the exchange in life. This 'exchange' was something I would always continue to apply, because it enabled me to keep learning. It let me evolve. I needed to evolve in order to ensure I would survive. Life, no matter what is happening, has a constant exchange of learning. Everyone learns differently and everyone changes differently.

When we meet people, if we accept and allow the purity of their souls to emerge, if we really look for this, we can then truly understand the possibility of exchange. It can open doors for us. Everyone has something to teach. Embrace it all, good or bad, and we can see clearly. I believe strongly in the power of exchange to define self-actualization. There are lessons all around us, and it's up to us to extract and apply them. My grandfather once said, "Wake up every day and learn something, because you can't go through life thinking you know everything. The day you stop learning is the day you die." I began to think that great learners in life gain fulfillment in their hearts. I always seemed to spend my days thinking ahead, but sometimes, this led me to negative thoughts. So I would then try and live in the moment to get out of the paradox, focus on the present, and engage myself in what I was doing. At times I would choose logic over emotions because my emotions were leading me, and that wasn't always the best thing. At times I learned to survive through logic, and this kept me in a good place. No matter what we are doing, or who we are with, we can always learn, and therefore an exchange will take place if we allow it.

I decided that true thought came when I was alone. My thoughts could be untainted by the pressure of people or the world around me. I wanted to listen to unfamiliar sounds of the earth, and voices stirring in the wind. If I listened carefully, I was in tune with my best thoughts. My true thoughts came back to me like I was holding a magnet to metal. One Saturday I found myself walking for a length of time. I arrived at a field and sat down in the grass. The wind blew and the clouds moved fast above me. The sky was clear in its blue colour and the movement of the earth was part of me, driving me through time. I looked down at the earth and back up to the sky. The environment in which we are able to live can be more remarkable than life itself. Nature's timing and rhythm, that gave me the ability to live, was amazing. Those who keep learning stay in sync with the world, while those who do not are left standing alone. In spite of what my experience had taught me, what was it that gave me the ability to keep learning? This very idea was real learning to me. I realized that we don't own the earth; it owns us. Being intuitive to this understanding helped me learn, grow, and let the world flourish around me. What I would do with my life was a time stamp. Each moment was something I couldn't do over. I had one life and one chance at it. It wasn't age that defined me, but the process of thought that carried me through time as if time didn't exist.

Life, with reflection, creates opportunities disguised as learning. Learning was what enabled my passion to grow, which in turn allowed my soul to grow. It's what allowed me to make a connection of my fear in traumatic events as a child, to the fear in my daily life. There are so many components, pieces, and parts to the world and our minds that we cannot ever begin to realize in their entirety. Not in one lifetime anyway. I needed to keep learning. Philosophy played a big part in my life, simply because it placed my mind in truth and dream at the same time. When I took the time to seek thought, I learned. Every time chaotic events occurred in my life, it seemed as though it was more of the same, but what I actually learned each time was something new. I also knew that my ability to recover from life's unfortunate events enabled me to learn and grow.

I needed to simply observe life, not judge it, and by doing this, I would learn.

2002

Actualize

I walked heavily in the snow, treading aimlessly through the woods. It was getting dark, and each falling snowflake winked past my face with a quick gleam of light. I was startled for a second. "Where are you heading to?" said the boy. "You really scared me," I said. "I am heading home...I think." The young boy looked up through the trees and looked back at me and asked, "The snowflakes, where are they coming from?" I looked up at the sky and told him the source was the clouds. As he started walking on, his last comment stood still in the cold, "I think they come from someplace else. Have you ever really looked at them?" I watched the boy as he walked away, vanishing in the distance. I looked back up at the sky and looked at the snowflakes falling, but this time I truly looked at them.

It was 8:09 in the morning and I awoke with the sun gently warming my face. "Hey man, what's up?" my roommate asked. I paused briefly and then replied, "Gotta head down to the store." "Want to grab breakfast?" he asked. "Nah, not today, I gotta get moving." I stepped out onto the street, looked at a big tree swaying in the wind, and started walking. I bumped into a woman as she was walking past. "Sorry," I said, but she ignored me and didn't seem fazed. As I passed more people on my way, they seemed to be in a better mood than I was. I began to smile at people, however not too many smiled back. The smiles that came back to me lifted my spirits, and I kept going. I stepped into a shop and went to the counter. "Hi, just want to grab some wild flowers, thanks." "How much are you thinking, we have a smaller bouquet that's around twenty dollars and another around twenty-five and some even as high as forty," the store attendant said. "Uhhh, doesn't really matter, but I want to pick them out myself, please," I responded. It was the anniversary of my grandfather's death and I was to make a trip down to the waterfront near the hospital where he had died. I made my way through downtown, then past the university and the hospital. I finally arrived at the water. Looking across the lake, I could see an island. The trees along the rocks were large and sparse and behind me there was a gazebo filled with Tai Chi enthusiasts. I placed the flowers between the rocks. I looked across at the hospital, and there on the top floor was the window of my grandfather's room overlooking where I stood. I knew he was gone, but I would never let him go. He was in my soul, my spirit, and my thoughts. I realized through the actualization of his life that he was going to live within me for eternity. Paying tribute to my grandfather every year also helped me recognize he was gone, and I could accept it. I closed my eyes and took in a deep breath, told him I would be back soon, and began walking home.

I recognized how my life had transpired and I could easily lay blame on others, but I wanted to keep looking within. I had to point the finger at myself only. I had many faults. I was not perfect, and most times I was not someone I would want others to emulate. I was learning to be real through self-actualization.

I wanted to understand myself dynamically, and then in turn be able to do something about it. My thought processes were sometimes poisonous; I pulled women into my life and then put up walls very fast so I wouldn't get hurt in these relationships. My thoughts led me to believe I didn't deserve good things in my life. I shut off from the outside world. I pushed through, logging my hours, and dragging myself around. In most cases I was a good actor, and I found that my soul was somewhere I was not. Most times I was a walking contradiction.

I needed to understand what had happened to my mental state from growing up in that environment. I had to dig deep and actualize. I recognized a number of things along the way. I began to recognize a bunch of weird idiosyncrasies and personality traits that I had developed. I knew that I internalized most things in my life, and that I could collapse and suffer mentally. I struggled with confidence, understanding who I was, and who I should be. I had to curve my adrenaline in every situation that held potential conflict. Seeing people on the street argue shook my adrenaline, as my body prepared for trauma. I would lie in bed, hearing neighbours argue, and my adrenaline would kick in. My body would tremble and shake as though I was naked in the snow. To reduce the stress, I needed to constantly remind myself that there was no danger. My mind needed to re-program cognitive skills, and try and objectively understand people's inflection, tone, demeanour, and body language, because I was always assuming I would be involved in conflict. When I self-actualized I realized my mind played tricks on me, analyzing words people used in conversation, wondering if there were negative implications, then closing off to the world because I felt rejected. I felt embarrassed by people's actions because they were foreign to me. I was embarrassed of excitement others would show, and then my actions would lead to more embarrassment. I had lived my life a certain way for so many years that when I was asked to do something that seemed normal to someone else, I would become uncomfortable. A hug would make me uncomfortable or embarrassed. It was like trying to be left handed after twenty years of being right handed. It was difficult, awkward, and embarrassing to adjust because I had learned violence, isolation, and fear. So what was normal for everyday people was an exhausting struggle for me, every day of my life. I felt I had to keep protecting myself and watching my back in an environment of conflict and broken trust, as I had done growing up, rather than depend on my parents for mutual respect and safety. I realized I needed to re-program my way of thinking. I realized I needed to change my thought processes in order to escape those harsh realities.

I had become an actor. I didn't want people to know me, so I had created something that prevented people from getting close. The challenges of simply being human were immense. I needed to constantly actualize so that I was aware of these things.

No one moment in my life defined me or made me think a certain way. It was an accumulation. It was a series of events, thought processes, and emotions. The neurons that fired in my head through calculated thoughts and restraint defined who I was going to be. I recognized that the events around me were affecting me and what I did was alter my thoughts to take me on a path away from my surroundings. At times the dark places owned me. They brought me deep into anger and sorrow. My mind needed to create something new. I knew I needed to distance myself from the past in order to find that. So, I came to terms with distancing myself from my mother for a while. I knew it had to be done. I wrote her a letter.

Dear Mom,

Well, I am sure you know I am doing fine. My work is good and my life is filled with busy days. I still go to the gym and play basketball recreationally. It's amazing how time seems to fly by. I needed time to reflect on the past events in my life. I need you to understand why I made this decision to create space between us, which was absolutely the hardest decision I've ever made. I will attempt to explain it and I need you to attempt to understand the best you can. Some of it may seem harsh, or some of it may hurt you, but this is the best way I know how to tell you.

Through the past years, growing up, I never deny or block out what we all went through. This made me who I am today. My childhood was really me being an adult. I do praise you for being the mother you were and who you attempted to be while going through everything. Many of my qualities I attribute to you. You taught me a lot of my values and morals. My humanistic nature and my spiritual side both came from you. My manners and etiquette came from you. My humility came from you. However, over the years I saw you live a life that wasn't for me. I wouldn't be where I am today if I hadn't separated myself from it. And in all honesty my past still haunts me, and I continue to deal with it. I have never used my past as an excuse and have always been grateful for what I have in my life. I always remember there is worse out there. I will always without doubt try and put others first, but this time I come first. I am surrounded by good people, and positive things. I am in an environment that is drug free, alcohol free, and free of violence. That is all my choice. I only want what is good in my life, goodness that will contribute to the growth of my mind and body.

It destroyed me every time you called me upset, beat down, or running into problems. You were in and out of the hospital, and it was so painful to watch this. After visits to see you I would leave and cry. You seemed to be encapsulated by a series of bad events I thought you would never get out of. This did not let me function properly. My anxiety increased and it was not healthy. I need to tell you my side to it all. I need to tell you about the demons and the hate, the sadness and all the hurt along the way through all those years. I chose a different path than you and Dad. You are both remarkable people. But I wanted something different and still do. I know I am meant for something good in life. I miss you, but I needed to distance myself for a while. I didn't know for how long but I knew I needed to. My view is this: No matter where I turned, there was violence, whether it was at our home or my father's home, and there were always drugs and alcohol. When you are young, and you live in that world, it takes you away from your studies and it positions you to deal with real life. I missed out on being the smart ass, intelligent, know it all kid I was early in public school. I needed parental leadership in my life, not chaos. When you have your parents turn their backs or follow a bad path, it's hard to trust; it's hard to accept that people love you and want to be around you. It's hard to push forward and know that everything in life will be okay. I understand now that life has a tension. We want one thing but are destined for another. I saw so much potential in you before you became ill. You were the motivation and inspiration in my life.

My sister and I started a new life with you, one that was promising and positive. Then you were gone, without you knowing it. Again, this is my view. And it is real to me, so I need you to understand where I am coming from. At that time, when I moved to Dad's for college, it was a horrible experience with his drinking and it felt like I had nowhere to turn. Sure, I got into some bad things, but I soon realized I am better than that. I want to hold my head up with confidence in who I am and what I am about in life. I wanted to talk to you about my feelings and how I felt as a child, but you chose to get angry with me. You chose to laugh, saying that I was so dramatic, but I remembered those things vividly. Or when we talked on the phone, your excuse was for me to take medication or get help. I needed to talk, with my mother, but my life is lived differently than yours and it feels as if you never recognized that. I want to live my life looking back and remembering the good things, not the bad. The anger is gone, and it has been replaced with understanding, forgiveness, and acceptance. I believe I have a beautiful soul and that you helped me create it. You once had a beautiful soul as well, but it's been so long since I have seen it in you. It was hard watching you go through so many bad times and bad events. They drained you.

However, I hear that you are becoming more yourself now and that you are becoming healthy. I will see you at sister's wedding. I want to focus on her and nothing else there. I know for a fact that I have not written everything that's in my mind. Maybe someday soon we can sit down and talk. Just you and me. Maybe we can go out to the cottage and talk there. Out by the water.

I am doing well. I am healthy from what I know. And I have a love for life and the beauty it has to offer. I don't want to be a part of the chaos anymore. Life will always be ups and downs, without a doubt. That's what life is, learning experiences, and I look forward to growing and learning until I am old. I do want us to share in each other's lives, but I want to share more good than bad. And we haven't done that in the past ten years.

You are always on my mind, every day. I never forget about you or block you out. I just need time to heal. I am still dealing with things, and continue to do so every day. I continue to relive the past at times. I will not just move on and get over it. I will embrace it and learn from it. I will let the past create a better me. For us to move on in our relationship, we need to understand where each other comes from, appreciate what each of us has gone through, and how we feel. I know you've had plenty of hardships, but don't forget, your children were alongside a lot of it. I know you are better than that and I know you deserve a beautiful life. Don't ever think you don't.

I will see you soon Mom.

Love, Zechariah

Sometimes I had to become selfish. Instinctually, I had to be selfish through all those events in order to survive. I became selfish as a child trying to survive, and this poured over into my adult life. Sometimes I would forget to shut it off, and it was certainly a detriment. I had to carry myself through the illusion just to be normal through the day, pretending to be happy. This carried with me, and now I needed to understand the boundaries of being overly selfish so that it wouldn't affect other aspects of my life. When I became more aware of these through self-actualization, I found a better reality that I could alter, change, and re-direct. But understanding who we are through being real with ourselves can take years, and sometimes never happen at all. It takes observation and immense patience. It takes receiving criticism and feedback from those around us, and we need to be completely open, but not lose ourselves in the process. I would walk through doors of perception. I thought that if my parents could let me down and turn their backs, then others in my life would almost certainly do the same. So, based on who I was talking to, I would close off and become an actor. I became what I perceived they wanted me to be.

By actualizing, I was able to grow. I needed to always be in tune with my opportunities for self-actualization. I needed to always be aware, and open to my opportunities as a human. When I actualized, I became accountable and I owned my life through the responsibility of me and me only. Understanding ourselves is never easy, and sometimes never happens at all. I was fortunate to understand myself to some degree through a defining truth. I knew that truth would become clear when I would actualize.

2003

Appreciate

The young boy stood at the crosswalk and stared across the street. I thought to myself, just go, but no, I should wait in order to set an example for the boy. He looked at me, and then I looked both ways for traffic. There was nothing. "I want to cross the street but I have to wait for the sign," he said to me. "You probably should," I responded. "Seems that these signs are road blocks to thinking." I always wondered about the impact of society's expectations on people. Does society provide people with peace, or is it something we fight against, trying to instead create our own? Society suggestively guides us into the status quo. It wants us to fit our narrow thoughts into a tight little box with confining boundaries. It has borders we cannot always see, but certainly feel. If we do anything outside the status quo, we are looked at differently. If we don't get a job, raise a family, or find ourselves paying rent, society is thrown a curveball. Society lends a structure, almost forgotten, to each of our lives. To me, society seems to be a scripted movie. But how are we able to appreciate if everything is already there, waiting, laid out in a script we've already read?

The plane landed around 9:09 in the morning, February ninth. It was a five hour trip that seemed to go by in an hour. When I stepped off the plane, the climate was warm, dry, and unquestionably distant from my own world. People smiled, cheered, and greeted me with open arms. I made my way across the landing strip, through the airport, onto the bus, and over to the resort. There was open land, hills, and cabins up at the top. Along the hill were pools and restaurants, and at the bottom, of course the ocean. I stood out on the restaurant patio at the top of the hill and looked out over the water. Small islands and water as far as I could see were what my mind took in. The air was cool and brisk. It filled my lungs with freedom.

The first morning of my trip, I started walking aimlessly down a road. I saw a cab driving quite fast. "Hey. Over here!" I yelled, waving my arms. He saw me, and skidded to a stop. I hopped in the backseat. The driver spoke English. "Where you headed my man?" he asked. "How about the nearest town?" I suggested. "Where you from yo?" I sat up in my seat and responded, "A faraway place, that's for sure." Along the way you could see small houses made from mud and branches. My ignorance led me to wonder if people actually lived in these huts. And there he was. A child. He walked out of his ten by ten dirt floor house. Correction, he walked out of his home. You could easily see on his face, this was his home he was so proud of. He looked up and smiled as I whipped past. He seemed so happy with so little. Or maybe he was so happy with so much that I couldn't see it. Amazing. I looked out the cab window at this young boy so full of life. He was full of peace, but more so, appreciation. The whole scene was in slow motion and I felt like I had been standing beside him. It's what we all should do; we should all appreciate every day, our surroundings and all that we have. I had learned to appreciate things, especially the relationships in my life. After I saw this boy, I immediately reflected and understood the value of what I had in my life. Is this what appreciation is?

When I got back home, I was back in the real world. As much as I appreciated being home, I was back into a society that took things for granted, a society that moves so fast. It just keeps building with pressure, materialism, and a sacrifice of health along the way. I started thinking about how we take things for granted and stress about silly things, like our next house, car, or shoes, while there are people across the world searching for clean drinking water every single day. Society now seemed to be so far removed from humanity, and the compassionate, helping, enduring spirit of people was dwindling. It was removed from looking out for others, and simply saying please and thank you to the people around us. This made me sad and appreciative at the same time.

I knew my life was filled with good things and I appreciated them. It's just that most times all the chaotic events were so powerful that they masked what was good. I started to reflect on each event that happened in my life and appreciate how I survived, rather than bathe in the horror. I started to wonder how the impact of these events would change me in society. As life moves forward without looking back, we tend to get caught up in such a blaze of change and drama that isn't ours. I learned that life represents personal value, not stature or wealth. Why would I judge someone based on their status of what they did for work, what house they have, or what car they drive? I needed to remember that the life people presented to me was not necessarily the life they lived behind closed doors. Maybe they went home and played the piano brilliantly, or maybe they were amazing at something else in their life that I didn't know about. Maybe they were just an amazing person who always put others first, who always loved their children, and who always believed in doing the right thing. I decided that I needed to understand something thoroughly in life before I formed my opinion, and even then, I needed to be compassionate in doing so. In the big picture we are all the same creatures, travelling in a direction that no one really knows. We need to create our own purpose, which will then unfold into appreciation. I continued to see a therapist to talk about the events in my past and to find a way to always stay ahead of the demons. I was diagnosed with post traumatic stress disorder and deemed to have some social anxiety. Most people look for an ending, but I accept that it won't ever end. Would society accept me? Would I be labeled as someone with a mental disorder or as someone 'different'? I couldn't help but feel that life was very much a façade when I was out in society. I was determined to reconfigure the societal DNA laid out in front of me.

It was a Sunday at around 10:11 in the morning when I got asked to lunch at the restaurant across the street from where I lived. "I think I will get the seafood platter," I said to the others. When the food arrived, I began to eat, no pause, no rest, until the platter was gone. As I sat with a full stomach and talked with the others, I started to sneeze. "Shit, my allergies are early this year," I said. I sneezed again. And then I sneezed again. Soon after, I started to feel my leg itch. "Gotta go blow my nose, be right back," I said to the others. I went to the washroom and my eyes were red. I went back to the table and mentioned to everyone that I needed to head home to get allergy pills. I paid and left. I entered my apartment and from the couch my roommate looked over at me. "Whoa, what happened?" he said. "Is it bad?" I asked. "Did someone punch you in the eye?" my roommate said jokingly. "Nah, I just had lunch and started sneezing." I made my way up to the washroom and looked into the mirror. This time my right eye was almost shut. "Heading to the hospital," I said quickly to my roommate as I ran down the stairs. "Want me to go with?" he said. "I'm fine," I answered. Along the way I could feel my body staggering a bit, my walk was slowing, and I met up with a man holding out his hat asking for change. "Hey man, can you spare some....never mind, sorry," he said. I just waved and kept walking. My body became more difficult to control and I resembled a drunk who just been released from a bar. My breathing became shallow. As I got close to the hospital it was if I had been slipped acid in my drink. I walked into the entrance and sat down as soon as I could see a chair. "Are you having an allergic reaction?" the nurse asked. I nodded. When I woke up, I was laying on a hospital bed. An IV was plugged into my hand and three nurses were standing around me. My shirt was off and I asked what happened. "You passed out in the waiting room," the first nurse said. "We gave you two shots of adrenaline, some prednisone, and an IV. Thirty seconds longer and you would have collapsed on the street. We are trying to get your hives down so you should be a few more hours here. We can't let you go until they're gone." I thanked them all and lay there, drained and a bit confused. A couple hours went by and I found myself looking over at an empty chair. I wondered why anaphylaxis had now become part of my life. I also wanted to go piss really badly. Seven hours went by and I kept looking at that chair. It was empty the whole time. There was no one to sit and wait with me. There was no one to make me feel as though I was not alone. A few days later I returned, this time with a card of thanks for all the nurses. When I walked back home, I thought about that empty chair. I hoped someday that the chair would have someone sitting in it, waiting and smiling back at me when I looked over. I knew I would appreciate being alive so much more.

A few months later, my family decided that they wanted to commemorate my grandfather by planting a tree in his memory, at the cottage my grandmother called home. We called it a commemoration but it went deeper than that; it was a family reunion. I believed that for all of us it was a goodbye. A car pulled up and my mother stepped out of the passenger side. I hadn't seen my mother for quite some time; I think maybe a year or two. When I saw her I had to step away. I walked to the back of the cottage and held back tears. She had changed. Her appearance had changed. But I still believed she was there underneath. I still believed in her. I gathered my composure and went back out to the group. My mother stood, weak in her stance, looked me in the eyes and took a deep breath, "Zechariah, ooohhhh, my son. You look so good. I've missed you so much," and she grabbed me and kissed my cheek. "Hi Mom, it's so good to see you, I missed you too," I responded. My mother and I stood beside each other, holding hands and just being in the moment. When I first saw her it seemed like she was not the same person, but her touch reassured me she was. We all stood around the place we would be planting the tree, each taking a turn with the shovel. We lifted the tree and placed it in its new home. As we packed the roots of the tree with soil I could see the happiness in my family. I could see everyone's eyes light up. We were accepting that the core of our family, my grandfather, was gone but not forgotten. We didn't just plant a tree, we planted a life. My grandmother stood watching, smiling and knowing that my grandfather would always be with her. And in that moment, I learned to truly appreciate.

As chaotic as my life could be in this world, it was the subtle footsteps forward that left a trail of appreciation. But I needed to recognize it. I could live a life filled with love, laughter, and peace. When I thought of my life in this way, I learned to appreciate.

2004

Hope

The young boy stared at me with great intensity. "I need to find the answer," he said, referring to a simple question he had just asked about hope. I couldn't come up with an answer so I asked why he even needed one. He said because if he didn't know then he would always wonder. I again asked the question of why. The boy stared at me, and then replied. "Because if I know the answer, I would then be able to teach my kids," he said. I told him that was the best reason I had ever heard. I smiled. Before we parted I told him that I thought he would make a great father, and to never stop asking questions in life, and to never lose hope.

Sometimes when faced with problems, I would think of the worst outcome that could possibly happen. Mark Twain once said, "I have been through a lot of horrible things, to which most of them never happened." I knew that a negative result was mostly fictional in my mind. But I also knew that life is so precious that a simple decision, thought, or action can alter the course of one's life. That scared me.

I couldn't give love to others while caught in a depression or a violent memory. I needed to be real with myself. I needed to be aware. I realized I was angry, sad, tired, and lonely. The sadness ate at me. I realized I could be alone in this world. The events in my life were wearing away my spirit. I had been beaten, I had been tormented, and I had been dragged through hell.

I also realized that my decisions could hold the warmth of the sun. My energy flowed with the attitude I chose and life moved forward with every hand held. What remains is the collective perseverance, and those who choose to smile through it all.

Life has no choice but to progress through both success and failure. Our choice is what we decide to do with it. I had always searched for peace, and had found only traces. My life was never extraordinary, but it was certainly becoming more amiable. My life went in the direction that I chose, or maybe it went the direction that it was destined to go. My ethics were intact to help me discover reality in life.

Louis L'amour described a man's life as shaped first by environment, heredity, and the movements and changes in the world. He explained that there comes a time when it is in a man's control to shape his own life into what he wanted to be. Only the weak blame parents, their race, their times, their lack of good fortune, and fate. We have the ability to decide what we would be today, and what we would ultimately be tomorrow. This idea formed my understanding that I had to own my situation, thoughts, and actions at all times. My life, as I now understood it, was full of new beginnings. I didn't get set back; I started fresh and new with more knowledge, wisdom, and strength to overcome.

We are all in this together. We are in this world together through every turn in our lives. I realized I was inspired by helping others. When I gave to others, I made sure people realized that they were not alone. I realized a truth in giving to others; I realized I had friends and I realized they also provided growth in my life through the exchange. It seemed to me that the world was silent about these events my family went through. The world seemed void of passion to fix what my family went through. Family was now a realized need in my life. I was willing to move forward in order to build a family of my own, and be the change I wanted to see.

I realized I would soon be twenty-seven. What is it about age that defines us at times? Why do people ask our age, seemingly so curious, needing to know so they can then determine if we are of wisdom or not? One early morning I encountered a man on the street who was insistent on making conversation with me. "Hello there, good day it is." "Yes it is," I replied. "And where are you going in such a hurry?" he quipped. "Well, I am heading to work," I replied back, like he was out of his mind. Where else would I be heading on a Tuesday morning? "Well, don't forget to stop and breathe," he finally said. "Well, if I could stop here, I would stop for sure, however I can't, and I have a busy day ahead of me." "Well son, you see, life is all around us, in many forms. I know it's strange, but you enabled me to breathe today," he said, with a spring in his step. I finally made eye contact, smiled, and told him he had made my year. *Quite a simple gesture*, I thought. But did I have time to "breathe?" Did I realize that the weight of life itself can push me down depending on what I choose to carry? Did I ever realize the impact others had in my life, or did I even realize the impact I had on others? Did I really care about my job title, possessions, or even the clothes I wore? Did I truly see the beauty in life? It was true; I needed to find beauty in everything through my life - the people, the environment, and most important, my thoughts. I needed to breathe more freely. I'd better make time to see the true beauty in life and I'd better do it soon. Nobody knows for sure when our lives will end. I didn't take the time to realize that the weeds in my life had become flowers, and I was the one who had made it happen. At times it seemed that there was a dark cloud over my life and I couldn't see the light through it. I realized I was in control all along, and it felt great. What else could I accomplish? What else could I do with this power of changing weeds into flowers? I wanted to find out. I wasn't to be ashamed of my past, but proud of the person I had become, because of my past.

On September ninth I awoke at 9:11 in the morning, and sat up in my bed. I smiled, and there was a new aura about my attitude and my life. My wisdom had led me to this moment. The love from others had helped me and my soul had guided me. This I finally knew.

I walked into the bathroom and looked in the mirror. This time, instead of seeing the young boy who had always asked so many questions, I saw myself as the man I had become. I then asked myself a final question. "How much longer am I going to live the same life?" I stood and looked into my eyes, paused for a brief moment to look down at my hands, and then back at the mirror to see the scars which remained on my face, arms, and head. Carved into my body, they would forever be reminders. They would be life's tattoos and trophies. I knew I was a product of my own thoughts. I could never stop learning, and I would never stop growing. My eyes widened and my face relaxed, and then it hit me. I realized I would actualize the childhood I once knew. The pieces I had decided to remember had kept me trapped and confined, and mostly restricted to one thought process. I was confined to the paradox. The very framework around my life was old, needing replacement.

It was time, and I knew it. It was time to change, and time to feel the sun shining on both sides of my face. The warmth was coming and I knew it. It was just a matter of time before I made the first step. It didn't mean that my past was obsolete; it only meant I had embraced a new found acceptance of my past, and all the learning it had given me. I would appreciate the life I lived rather than choose to fight it. My life events provided exchange, strength, growth, and the ability to look at the world from so many angles. I knew that my life's harmony would come when my thoughts and actions were in sync.

I never stopped believing in who I was able to become. Over the years I gathered knowledge to succeed and overcome. My mother taught me about hope, but I used to think it was false. When realizations came to light throughout my life, hope shined brighter for me. I realized I had survived through continued hope. I realized that my past was blurred, and I also realized I had known that for quite some time.

So now, into the new day, hope was alive in me. I took my first deep breath and I knew I was awake. Everything was in focus.

Conclusion

Life isn't easy. It never will be. Nor does it have to be lived any particular way. We need to let down the walls around us and step out into the world. We need to choose a path of fulfillment. Zechariah's way of life is not absolutely right or perfect in any way, but rather the unfolding of a puzzle experienced by many in the world. Our lives can be significant or insignificant, depending on what we choose. Zechariah understands that each of us should live with core principles. We should each have personal building blocks to strengthen who we are. These provide clarity and structure to help guide us in tough times. Whether we choose religion, spirituality, both, or neither, that is up to us. But to lay a foundation to the way we live is vital. Here are the main building blocks that Zechariah accumulated over twenty-three years of his life. It isn't easy to assemble these blocks, and it's not always easy to live by them. We can rise up each day knowing that we can overcome, regardless of the result. It's important to stand up and be proud of our lives no matter what paths they have taken. Life's journey can be what we want. We just have to build it.

Twenty-Three Building Blocks:

Aware
Ethics
Reality
Attitude
Failure
Peace
Amiable
Strength
Overcome
Truth
Friends
Growth
Passion
Family
Health
Sacrifice
Wisdom
Love
Soul
Learn
Actualize
Appreciate
Hope

About the Author

Ryan R. F. Wilkinson is an emerging author, an artist, and a continuous learner of life's lessons. Ryan lives in Ontario, Canada. He can be reached at: ryan.r.f.wilkinson@gmail.com

Proceeds from this book will be donated to various organizations which support women and children in their journeys of overcoming domestic violence.

Made in the USA
San Bernardino, CA
19 December 2017